Catalina Vallejo

Plurality of Peaces in Legal Action

MASTERS OF PEACE

edited by the

UNESCO Chair for Peace Studies
of the University of Innsbruck / Austria

UNESCO Chairholder:
Wolfgang Dietrich

Volume 7

tirol Unser Land · universität innsbruck · UNESCO United Nations Educational, Scientific and Cultural Organization · UNITWIN Twinning and University Networks

LIT

Catalina Vallejo

Plurality of Peaces in Legal Action

Analyzing Constitutional Objections to Military Service in Colombia

LIT

Bibliographic information published by the Deutsche Nationalbibliothek
The Deutsche Nationalbibliothek lists this publication in the Deutsche Nationalbibliografie; detailed bibliographic data are available in the Internet at http://dnb.d-nb.de.

ISBN 978-3-643-90282-5

A catalogue record for this book is available from the British Library

Zweigniederlassung Zürich 2012
Klosbachstr. 107
CH-8032 Zürich
Tel. +41 (0) 44-251 75 05
Fax +41 (0) 44-251 75 06
e-Mail: zuerich@lit-verlag.ch
http://www.lit-verlag.ch

LIT VERLAG Dr. W. Hopf
Berlin 2012
Fresnostr. 2
D-48159 Münster
Tel. +49 (0) 2 51-620 320
Fax +49 (0) 2 51-23 19 72
e-Mail: lit@lit-verlag.de
http://www.lit-verlag.de

Distribution:
In Germany: LIT Verlag Fresnostr. 2, D-48159 Münster
Tel. +49 (0) 2 51-620 32 22, Fax +49 (0) 2 51-922 60 99, e-mail: vertrieb@lit-verlag.de

In Austria: Medienlogistik Pichler-ÖBZ, e-mail: mlo@medien-logistik.at

In Switzerland: B + M Buch- und Medienvertrieb, e-mail: order@buch-medien.ch

In the UK: Global Book Marketing, e-mail: mo@centralbooks.com

In North America: International Specialized Book Services, e-mail: orders@isbs.com

TABLE OF CONTENTS

SERIES EDITORS' FOREWORD 7
FOREWORD BY RACHEL SIEDER 9
PREFACE 11
ACKNOWLEDGEMENTS 15
TO WRITERS 17
INTRODUCTION 18

1. CONCEPTUAL FRAMEWORK: PLURALITY OF PEACES 34
Introduction 34
1.1 Preliminary Concepts 34
1.1.1 Positive and Negative Peace 35
1.1.2 Dimensions of Violence 36
1.2 The *One* Peace: Modernity 36
1.3 The Many Peaces: Postmodernity 39
1.3.1 European Postmodernity 40
1.3.2 Postmodernism's Key Contributions to Peace Studies 41
1.3.3 Postmodernity in Latin America 43
1.3.4 Energetic, Moral, Modern and Postmodern Peaces 46
1.4 *Transrational* Peaces 50
1.4.1 Apollo and Dionysius 51
1.4.2 Quantum Physics and Transpersonal Psychology 52
1.4.3 Twisting the Peaces 53
Conclusion 54

2. ROLE OF PEACE IN LEGAL THEORY AND PRACTICE 56
Introduction 56
2.1 What is Law? 57
2.1.1 Structural, Functional and Value-System Perspectives on Law 58
2.1.2 Classic Ideas on Law: Iusnaturalism and Iuspositivism 62
2.1.3 Tamanaha's Clusters of Meaning 64
2.1.4 Which are the actual laws to follow? 66
2.1.5 Perspective of the ONIC 70
2.2 Role of Peace in Legal Theory and Practice 71

2.3 Legal Type of Peace: the Modern ... 74
2.3.1 Social Peace vs. Inner Peace? ... 76
2.3.2 Legal Education as Training for Hierarchy ... 78
Conclusion ... 82

3. PLURAL PEACES VS. UNIVERSAL HUMAN RIGHTS ... 84
Introduction ... 84
3.1 Human Dignity and Denial of Full Humanity ... 84
3.1.1 Dehumanization and Pseudo-speciation ... 84
3.1.2 Indifference towards Death ... 85
3.2 Pseudo-speciation by use of Language in Colombia ... 87
3.3 Rights: Rejection of Pseudo-Speciation Narratives ... 88
3.4 Universal Human Good? ... 90
Conclusion ... 93

4. PLURALITY OF PEACES IN LEGAL ACTION ... 95
Introduction ... 95
4.1 Conscientious Objections to Military Service ... 96
4.1.1 Origin and Meaning ... 96
4.1.2 Colombian Conscription System ... 98
4.1.3 Jurisprudence before 2009 ... 99
4.1.4 The Violence involved in 'National Solidarity' ... 102
4.1.5 Pseudo-speciation of Objectors ... 104
4.1.6 Need for Transformation: Why some Decide to Object in Colombia? ... 107
4.2 Petition of Unconstitutionality ... 112
4.3 Decision C-728/09: Variations on Peace and Rights ... 115
4.3.1 Energetic Perspectives ... 116
4.3.2 Moral and Modern Perspectives ... 121
4.3.3 Postmodern Perspectives ... 123
4.3.4 Transrational Perspectives ... 130
4.3.5 Change of Judicial Precedent ... 134
Conclusion ... 140

CONCLUDING REMARKS ... 142

REFERENCES ... 148

Series Editors' Foreword

Starting from a profound personal unease with the question of the compatibility of plural peaces and national peace and solidarity, Catalina Vallejo innovatively opens up the whole area of legal studies towards transrational notions of peace. What interests her is how much leverage legal practitioners and scholars have in the constant emergence of many peaces in face of receiving, reviewing, considering, acting and ultimately giving right to conscious objectors to military draft in Colombia, a country characterized by intense and multiple expressions of violence. The main tenet of this work is that there already is a transrational turn in juridical discourses that discloses the nuances of many (legal) peaces, which challenge, provoke and ultimately transform the idea of a secure national peace.

In exploring these issues, Vallejo raises broader theoretical questions about legal readings, if and how legal interpretations and usages can speak the many peaces. In a detailed manner, she focuses on the concrete Constitutional revision of the compulsory military draft, for which she weaves a sound trans-disciplinary conceptual framework indicating her firm grasp of a large body of theoretical peace, conflict and security studies literature, combining those insights with critical legal discourses from a variety of interrelated and relevant perspectives. The book proceeds with the controversial issue of the universality of human rights from the angle of plural peaces. Vallejo does not restrict her analysis to the demand of unconstitutionality of Constitutional decisions, but eloquently and thoroughly puts forward how representatives from the State, civil society and particular interest groups make use of diverse peace narratives to resist, provoke and challenge the official discourse of national peace and solidarity based on the compulsory military draft.

The way Vallejo summarizes the interventions of the above-mentioned representatives, in conjunction with insights derived from the conceptual framework investigations, pays tribute to the creativity that ought to characterize peace practitioners and contributes with authenticity and sound academic work to foster transrational approaches in legal issues in a conflict setting.

It is refreshing to see work that consciously builds on existing frameworks in both a critical and creative manner. This publication, however, goes further. It seeks to combine legal studies and transrational peace studies. Therefore, because of its high quality and innovation we have included this piece in our series of excellent MA thesis of Peace Studies. This decision is furthermore grounded in the conviction that the results of this work deserve to be discussed publicly. While firmly establishing that there already is a juridical turn in the concrete case under examination, Vallejo opens a new field of discussion: After the trans-rational shift in diplomacy, international peacekeeping, development cooperation and economy, do we find also a transrational turn in law? This text suggests so and acts as a suitable reminder that transrational peace approaches are —in fact— capable of engaging, integrating and, yes, ultimately twisting modern discourses on national peace towards many peaces. We thus make this thesis available to our readers in the hope of sharing a volume that comprehensively gives us the electrifying result that it is possible to live, think, feel and act many (legal) peaces.

With this text, Vallejo has opened a new field in the transrational debate and has become one of the leading voices of this direction in Peace Studies. Like earlier authors of the series Masters of Peace, Vallejo belongs to the circle of excellent alumni of the Innsbruck School, who do not just carry this approach around the globe, but also successfully integrate it into their own field of work. The editors welcome her as pioneer of the transrational peaces and elicitive conflict transformation and gladly take note how the young generation adapts and develops further this approach.

Wolfgang Dietrich and Josefina Echavarría A.
Innsbruck, October 2012.

FOREWORD

By Rachel Sieder

Since the early 1990s anthropologists have drawn our attention to the different ways in which universal concepts, such as human rights, security or peace, are understood by individuals and groups in diverse contexts across the world. Lawyers and legal scholars also engage with differentiated understandings of rights when they interpret the meaning of these abstract concepts within specific judicial settings. In recent years politics has become increasingly judicialized across Latin America as civil society groups look to the courts to shape government policies. Analysis of this judicialization of politics has included the study by many scholars of the innovative jurisprudence of Colombia's Constitutional Court, one of the most active and "rights-enforcing" high courts in the region. The Court has issued groundbreaking rights jurisprudence even while Colombia remains locked in an internal armed conflict which has lasted for decades and cost tens of thousands of lives.

In this book Catalina Vallejo focuses specifically on the Constitutional Court's 2009 ruling which allowed for conscientious objection to compulsory military service, challenging the highly controversial "democratic security" policy of then president Álvaro Uribe (2002-2010). Uribe's militarized policies divided Colombia's population into those who sided with the government and its conception of peace - which entailed all-out war-, and those who opposed it. Yet as Vallejo's analysis shows, hundreds of different organizations in Colombia rejected such a Manichean division and through a process of legal mobilization demonstrated the highly contested and pluralistic nature of concepts such as "security" and "peace". Ultimately opposition to compulsory military service before the courts stemmed from different understandings within Colombian society of what peace and security entails. Tasked with upholding and guaranteeing fundamental rights, the constitutional court justices played an interpretative role and in decision C-728/09 recognized objections to compulsory military service to be an essential component of the right to freedom of conscience, calling on the national congress to regulate its practice along with alternative (civil) forms of social service.

Vallejo argues that this decision demonstrates how Colombian constitutional justices came to accept pluralistic understandings of peace and human rights. In a wide-ranging literature review, she explores diverse conceptions of peace within philosophy, peace studies and sociology and considers how these pluralist understandings have come to be understood within law and legal reasoning. As she rightly states, "different perspectives on peace influence different argumentation of rights"; law is a social construction and norms and judicial argumentation reflect changes and dynamics within national and global society. Today in the face of the seemingly endless "war against terror" that seeks to divide the world into "them" and "us", her study is a timely reminder of the power that legal reasoning can play in defending diversity and promoting tolerance.

Rachel Sieder
Research Professor, Centro de Investigaciones y Estudios Superiores en Antropología Social (CIESAS), Mexico City.
Mexico City, October 2012.

PREFACE

This book explores if and how different interpretations of peace affect legal discourses and practices, concretely those concerning the exercise of rights. By building on the idea that there are various and many times contradictory interpretations of *peace* in history and culture (Dietrich, 2012), I set out to examine how these many peaces interplay in legal spheres.

This study focuses on a 2009 Constitutional Court case in Colombia, where various civil society organizations demanded the revision of compulsory military draft for conscientious objectors. Before 2009 the Colombian legal system did not allow objections to military service or included alternative services of civil character. More than 400 organizations from different affiliations presented *amicus curiae* to the Court formulating a rich myriad of interpretations on the meaning of peace, solidarity, and the duty of military service. The case ruling (Decision C-728/09) recognized for the first time the possibility to object to military service, understood as part of the exercise of the right to freedom of conscience.

What makes this court case special for this study is that it ocurred during a time of heated war between the Colombian army, guerrilla groups and paramilitary forces (2002-2012). Notably, in 2003 the Colombian government had decided to win the political conflict against guerrillas by military means; consequently, it strengthened the state-armed forces, informed public policy with an understanding of peace out of security and enforced it to all Colombians by law.

Peace out of security is one of the many possible interpretations of peace by persons and groups in Colombia and elsewhere. It sees peace as a status of perfection in the future, when enemies have been defeated. From this perspective, the elimination of the contrary is a necessary condition for peace. Because the complex and long lasting Colombian armed conflict has had different effects in people, after the enforcement of the security policy in 2003 (Presidencia de la República y Ministerio de Defensa de Colombia, 2003), some persons and groups joined the military-based security effort in genuine agreement, and some others soon found themselves in a profound dilemma (War Resisters' International, 2009).

For persons and groups whose practices and traditions were mainly motivated by diverging interpretations —such as peace out of coexistence with the contrary, or peace as embodied experience— the mandate to join the military effort as means to national peace seemed not only irrational and physically repulsive, but also disrespectful of their right to freedom of conscience. Precisely in the midst of war the case was brought to court in 2008 and, interestingly, it served as one more platform to express, discuss and problematize diverging understandings of peace, security and solidarity in Colombia, as well as to propose structural changes to allow these perspectives to respectfully coexist.

Together with many other legal and social efforts to humanize and better understand the Colombian armed conflict, I believe that this concrete piece of jurisprudence (Decision C-728/09) —with the opinions, doctrines and interviews that it compiles— serves in part as documental memory of the Colombian war. It is a small but significant contribution to the full acknowledgement of the suffering experienced by all the parties to the conflict, as well as their intimate reasons to engage with or object to warfare.

The original manuscript of this book was written in 2010-11 as a dissertation for the Master's program in Peace Studies of the University of Innsbruck. It was part of a personal search towards better understanding the collective ideas (including my own) creating, sustaining, and permanently reshaping the protracted war in my home country, Colombia. Having a background in Legal Studies and a passion for constitutional processes, when designing my dissertation I wished to explore how the legal argumentation of fundamental rights is articulated to such collective ideas. While writing this book I was motivated by an understanding of *thought as action* (Grosz, 2001), meaning that our acts often reflect the way we think about phenomena. Therefore problematizing our thoughts *is* action, it allows social transformation.

By digging into the lines of the 2003 Colombian security policy, regulations on obligatory military service, and reading media articles on the armed conflict, I discovered the interplay of abstract discourses on peace and security stimulating violent and non-violent actions from all militias and their correspondent supporters and objectors in Colombia. In this book I try to describe how plural interpretations of peace informe one type of action: the legal action. Which is not less active for being legal. People go to court and also go to the battlefield, in the same way they type security policies, conscientious objection essays, *amici curiae*, or rulings: motivated and permanently accompanied by thought, ideas, perspectives.

My intention with writing this book is to contribute to a chain of thoughts about peace in plural, started many years ago by postmodern philosophers and peace researchers whose works I study in detail in the following chapters. Moreover, I aim to contend the idea that legal practices *only* allow the use of homogeneous ideas on peace and solidarity framed by the nation-state.

I attempt to show that courts and other legal institutions are, and are meant to be, platforms to perform and speak the many peaces.

I am writing this preface in September 2012. Today, the situation in Colombia is different from what it was in 2010 when I wrote my dissertation. Belligerent actions and political discourses are somehow different eventhough the armed conflict continues. Also I am different. The latest developments in the armed conflict (not mentioned in this book), such as the institutionalization of transitional justice mechanisms, the official recognition of an internal armed conflict of political character, the creation of the Victims and Land Restitution Law in 2011, and the recent chance given by the executive branch to a process of political negotiation with guerrillas[1] are some of the facts that have to be mentioned here and today make me appreciate much more the efforts made by the Colombian government than before.

Also, two very transformative experiences with Theater of the Oppressed and Theater for Living[2] after having submitted the dissertation influenced changes in the way I perceived war and aggression generally, and my absolute interpretations of 'wrongdoers' and 'victims' of the Colombian conflict concretely. Through theater practices I started to see the importance of acknowledging the needs and suffering of *all* persons and groups involved in the armed confrontation, including those with whom I express strong disagreement in this book. I cannot change the manuscript today, that would mean writing a new text, but I wish to honor their suffering and respect their intimate motivations to engage in warfare, even if I do not support them in that endeavor. I am being challenged by the idea that any peacebuilding process needs to consider the humanity and systemic motivations of all the parties to the conflict.

This year I had the opportunity to interview professor Iván Orozco Abad in Bogotá, who introduced me to the idea of "complex political victims" coined by Erika Bouris (2007). The concept is an analytical tool to address the substantial problems with the dichotomous conception of actors in a conflict, especially in cases of long civil wars, where the parties involved can be

---

[1] See *Ley de Victimas y Restitución de Tierras* [Victims and Land Restitution Law][(Law 1448/2011); *Transitional Justice and DDR: The Case of Colombia* (Jaramillo, S. and others, 2009; *Truth-Telling and Internal Displacement in Colombia* (Vidal-López 2012). For further reference.

[2] See *Theater of the Oppressed* (Boal 2000), *Theatre for Living: The Art and Science of Community-Based Dialogue* (Diamond, 2007). For further reference.

sometimes —and in Colombia, many times— oppressed as well as oppressors, victims as well as perpetrators.

I want to thank professor Orozco for sharing his ideas with me and in so doing challenging my judgements and making an important contribution to the analysis I started developing in this book, Elisabeth Grosz for her valuable elaborations on *thought as action* which I heard with enthusiasm in a conference in Bergen, Norway, last month and consider of most relevance for this work on plural ideas of peace in legal action. Special gratitude also to theater practitioners Héctor Aristizábal and David Diamond, and the theater groups formed in their workshops[3] for allowing me to me *feel* with and for the stranger, and comprehend by the use of arts what I could not see and feel by the use of rational methods only.

Despite these latest transformations of facts, discourses and in part of my perspective as author, apart from updating some sources, the content of the book remains mainly the same it was when I submitted it as a dissertation over a year ago. It is the living remembrance of a precious moment in a process of transformation.

Catalina Vallejo Piedrahíta
Bergen, September 2012.

---

[3] A workshop facilitated by Aristizabal took place in Bergen, in November 4-6, 2011, and another one was guided by David Diamind at the 54th International Conference of Americanists in Vienna in July 15-20, 2012. See *Theatre for Living* (Diamond 2007); *The Blessing Next to the Wound: A Story of Art, Activism, and Transformation* (Aristizabal & Lefer, 2010). For further reference.

ACKNOWLEDGEMENTS

I am the author of this book, but the text you have in your hands is not the result of my individual effort only. There is a group of people who made the whole process of designing the research proposal, writing the text and publishing it possible. From the bottom of my heart I want to express gratitud to:

The board, core facilitators and grup of students of the Peace Studies Program at the University of Innsbruck for their essential contributions to my process of problematizing and exploring concepts of peace, security, development and conlfict transformation. Moreover, for adding an 's' to make them plural and twisting them with the relational component that connects us all.

To Josefina Echavarría for her integral guidance and research supervision. Better than an excellent advisor who helps improving a text is an advisor who, in addition, cares about the human typing the text. Thanks to her, a project that seemed chaotic and impossible to finish turned into a great learning experience.

To my classmates and friends Noah Taylor and Alicia Dueck for their dedicated editions and constructive feedback to initial versions of this text. To fellow students and treasured friends Florencia Benitez-Schaeffer, Magiarí Díaz Díaz and Joanne Rossiwall for the fun and fruitful discussions that we had regarding the initial proposal, and for their love and support throughout the writing process. Very special gratitude to Shawn Bryant for the detailed and commited hard work he put into preparing this text for publication and for his encouragement when most needed.

To the Christian Michelsen Institute (CMI) in Bergen, Norway, where I wrote my dissertation, for providing me with the necessary tools to undertake this research, from a desk and necessary cups of coffee to a wide academic frame for discussion. Also, thanks a lot for financing the final copy-editing of this book. Special gratitude to Elin Skaar and Karin Ask for helpful comments to the initial manuscript, and to Siri Gloppen in general for always bringing out the best in people and concretely for srtongly supporting this project.

To the Rafto Foundation for Human Rights in Bergen, where I volunteered for some months while writing this book. The work and discussions around the organization of the Rafto Prize for Human Rights 2010 enriched my theoretical research on rights and dignity, allowing me to observe dynamics of structural violence and plural peaces in action.

To my partner, Josef Daniel Rasinger, for giving me the essential inspiration and support to start, continue, and finish this academic project. Thanks for your precious company both during the difficult dark times (metaphorically and literally! during the Norwegian winter) and precious moments of celebration.Your presence makes me wish for a new day.

Finally, immense gratitude to my family in Colombia, and specilaly to my parents Alyda and Hugo for their cheerful and respectful attitude towards all my endeavors. It gives me the confidence to undertake risks and enjoy learning processes like this one.

TO WRITERS

During the process of writing this book, I have realized what a sacrifice of one's own life it is to write an academic text. Leisure time is significantly reduced and replaced by mostly indoor, isolated, non-ergonomic reading and writing. Many chances to spend time with loved ones or to enjoy outdoor activities need to be sacrificed.

At the same time, systematically reading academic literature on the fields of Peace and Legal Studies made me transform many of the ideas I had before starting to write this book. By reading the analysis, opinions, and personal stories of other authors, I have been able to think in new ways and slowly develop more empathetic attitudes towards unfamiliar, the strange. Going through the literature to which I refer in this work has allowed me to expand my analytical framework and consequently to somehow experience a freer attitude in everyday life, one that is a little less resistant to otherness.

This is why today I want to symbolically thank the authors cited in this book and those from whom they learnt, for sacrificing their own leisure time in order to elaborate and write.

Introduction

The content of this book is my dissertation for the completion of the Master Program in Peace Studies at the University of Innsbruck, which is inspired by the United Nations Educational, Scientific and Cultural Organization (UNESCO) Manifesto 2000. Amongst the cornerstones of the Manifesto are: the respect the life and dignity of each human being, the practice of active non-violence and the defense of freedom of expression, cultural diversity and new forms of solidarity (Universität Innsbruck, 2011). In this book I explore the integration of those cornerstones into my previous background in legal studies, aiming to incorporate them into my personal life and professional practice.

The standpoint of the Master Program is based on the conclusion that beyond one peace there are many peaces, all of which are contextually grounded, that number as many as there are human perceptions in the world, consequently, the academic challenge is to analyze the relation between these myriad interpretations (Universität Innsbruck, 2011). According to this philosophical stance, the search for peace starts with the deconstruction of the observer's identity and the awareness of how one's own background shapes research processes. Thus students are particularly encouraged to start academic works with their personal perspective and use the style of writing in first person. This is the style I will use in this book.

Personal Perspective

Let us start this investigation by stating where my engagement with the study of structural violence comes from. I was born and raised in Medellín, Colombia, a city with the reputation of being one of the most violent in the world during the last decades, home town of several internationally persecuted drug lords, and center of violent dispute between mafias and organized criminal organizations. Medellín is a city with big gaps in terms of welfare opportunities amongst people and also a city of mountains, science, hard work, and arts.

I belong to a loving and diverse family from which I got to know both the dark and light sides of humanity. My mom and grandmother are good storytellers, therefore, since I was a child I have heard stories of many different types of people with whom I share blood bonds. For instance, there was a strict military man who, together with a group called *"junta militar"* served as president of the republic for a short period of time during a dictatorship in 1958. At the same time, there is the story of an activist woman, married and a loving mother of six, who dared to be the first woman to ride a bicycle and to wear pants in our small and rather conservative town back in the late 1940s. Once, she shaved her head because "it felt fresher," which caused a scandal amongst the macho leaders of the time. She engaged in politics and found ways of expressing her opinions and standing for the rights of women around her.

One of my grandfathers died before I was born, he is remembered for being a loving and supportive father, dedicated husband and successful entrepreneur; my other grandfather is recalled by my grandmother as an intelligent engineer and romantic man who would become violent when drinking and after the years forgot how to respect a woman and support his children. This is how she still recalls him today. He was a loving grandfather to me. Then a couple of generations back, there is a respected artist and the first woman publishing paintings of female naked bodies in Colombia. Because of her work, she received threats of excommunication[4] from the Catholic Church and was forced to shut down art exhibition in Franco's Spain in 1955. She is famous for picturing important historical political events that happened in Colombia during the years of her youth; she expressed her political opinions via painting. Known for her provocative art, she was interviewed at the age of 94 and when asked about how she would portrait her country in the present she said: *destruido, la gente matándose* (destroyed, people killing each other). I have the same opinion today, things do not seem to have changed much; cultures of violence seem to become wider and deeper.

In 2011, a museum-park is being built in honor of this activist painter. There she stands proudly amongst my ancestors along with two of my second cousins who, despite having had a family and the chance to study and work, were led by their story to drug addiction and a life in the streets of Medellín. One of them, who was an artist and a gifted painter as well, was an eccentric person and later on was sent to a sanatorium. The other cousin has been in jail for continuous violent episodes. Today, both names and faces are avoided by some of our relatives: they bring shame to many in the family.

I am connected by blood to all these people and many more. Some of them are remembered as heroes; others were victims of the socio-economic cir-

[4] Exclusion of the offender from all church fellowship (Bender, 1955).

cumstances of the country and ended up being excluded from their family and society. With all of them I share love bonds that persist beyond any rational explanation; we have a story together, we share our humanity in a very deep way. From my ancestors I know of arts, science and virtue, as well as of violence, suffering and guilt. All of them are equally meaningful to me; they all influence my personal story, worldview, and someway my interest in studying the structural aspects of violence. All of them had equal potential for good and evil, just like me.

From 2000 to 2005 I studied law at the *Universidad Autónoma Latinoamericana* and developed a strong interest in legal philosophy and public law, area in which I studied a specialization in 2006. I was also passionate about International and Human Rights Law.

There are many law faculties in Medellín; from where many people who currently serve as members of the government, judges, lawmakers and attorneys have graduated. Several presidents of Colombia have been lawyers, graduates from law faculties in Medellin as well. The argumentation and decisions made by these jurists every day as part of their legal practice strongly affect the lives of those involved in trials and also shape the political perceptions of the community as a whole and how the community chooses to manage power relations. From family issues to commerce and Human Rights, our legal practice is one of the elements forming the tapestry of moments of violence and peace occurring every day in Colombia.

Nowadays, I observe that many people are graduating as lawyers in my home city and, at the same time, I observe an endless situation of violence at all levels; there is inequality, irritation, blaming and revenge. I wonder what our contribution as jurists is to all this violence? Also, what is our contribution to social transformation and facilitation of moments of peace?

I practiced law in Colombia from 2005 to 2008, mostly in the fields of human rights education and administrative law. I worked for the local government of the city of Medellín for two years in the area of expropriation of land and real estate needed for the construction of new public schools and roads. During my short time of legal practice before starting my MA in Peace Studies, I dealt with people, legal argumentation, conflicts, communication, feelings, dis/satisfaction of human needs and negotiations. That short experience showed me that legal practice is a big challenge that definitely involves more than knowing the written law. It takes creativity and willingness to connect with people in their virtue as well as in their guilt and suffering.

Right on the very first day in the law faculty, I learnt that the supreme value and ultimate aim of law is *social peace*. According to my professors, law is created and used to avoid resorting to violence and to achieve peace for all.

Even though this statement was clearly made during the first year of classes, there was never further analysis on what peace is about. There was no discussion about our personal ideas of peace as law students or whether there is more than one/national manner of understanding and experiencing peace. We did not discuss what type of peace the law aims to create.

If peace is the aim of law, I wonder, when I use legal argumentation to give content to rights and norms in concrete legal cases, what kind of peace am I using as inspiration? Whose peace do I bear in mind? Is it the peace of my clients, my own idea of peace, or the national peace? Is it an international peace? Do we all experience peace the same way?

If taking into account a wider range of Colombian jurists —attorneys, legal representatives, judges, lawmakers, legal advisors, public prosecutors— how does the idea of peace that they bring to their legal practice influence structures of violence and peace in Colombia? During the course of my MA in Peace Studies, I had the chance to study in detail the side of law I could never explore in the law faculty: its deep connection to structural peace and violence. In this book, I attempt to explore the connections between the legal theory/practice and peace research, focusing on the specific case of the defense and security policy institutionalized in Colombia in 2002 (Presidencia de la República y Ministerio de Defensa de Colombia, 2003) that is increasingly driving people to object to military service by evoking diverging interpretations of peace and the right to freedom of conscience.

Research Problem

Lederach (1997) elaborates on the concept of *deeply divided societies,* explaining that they legitimate the use of armed force for reasons of defense. In resonance with Lederach's concept, Colombia is going through a deep cultural process of polarization created by the public defense and security policy enforced by the law.

This process started to take place in the frame of the Democratic Security Policy created by ex-president Alvaro Uribe in 2002 (Presidencia de la República y Ministerio de Defensa de Colombia, 2003). This policy aims to use military force to physically and politically exterminate non-state armed groups. Echavarría (2010) explains that this security policy feeds violence and by discourse it writes political identities in the Colombian people, such as 'the state', 'us' (the 'good Colombians') and 'them' (the 'terrorists' or 'bad Colombians'). Those categories are fed by cultural means: political ideologies, religion, language, arts and academia, in what Galtung calls *stereotyping* the other in the context of cultural violence (Galtung, 1990).

Following Hall (1996) Echavarría bases her argument upon the assumption that "discourses are *living texts,* they are not just mere 'linguistic artefacts' but rather have material effects, constructing and producing identity categories" (Echavarría, 2010: 18). In the same sense, by quoting Regehr, Lederach explicates the dynamics of *identity* conflicts:

> Identity conflicts emerge with intensity when a community in response to unmet basic needs for social and economic security, resolves to strengthen its collective influence and struggle for political recognition. Almost two thirds of the current armed conflicts can be defined as identity conflicts, and some estimates count as many as 70 current political conflicts worldwide that involve groups formally organized to promote collective identity issues. (Regehr in Lederach, 1997: 8)

As a Colombian, I can certainly feel the force of the identity conflict. I can also feel the pulling power of the political identities. Both when I am in the Colombian territory and abroad I feel as if I should radically take part in one of the sides of the armed conflict and give legitimation to the use of violence and separation that sustains the security policy. Not expressing strong opinions about how much 'they' deserve to die in military operations is now considered suspicious, even if one expresses dissent from the violent means of non-state armed groups.

In 2002 the security policy promised peace out of militarization. Surprisingly, instead of a system of one national peace, what can be found in 2011 is the escalation of some particular forms of violence (CNP, 2010; INMLCF, 2009). There has been an increase in the number of violent situations taking place at the grassroots, however bombings and massive kidnappings have decreased compared to numbers during the 1980s and 1990s. The identity conflict is everywhere. The security policy has legitimized cultures of disrespect and use of violence to exclude the dangerous 'other'. Acts of violence are rampant. As Echavarría points out:

> Once the security policy postulates are built-in to the daily behavior of citizens and shape their imaginings about peace and war, the oppressive and repressive violence of the state is no longer indispensible. 'We' have become our most feared security forces. There is no war front, nor is there a home front. This is a war waged everywhere —from shopping malls to telecommunications— and everyone is suspect. (Echavarría, 2010: x)

Rising Rates of Violence in Colombia

Evidence provided by the Colombian National Institute of Forensic Medicine (INMLCF) and the National Planning Council (CNP) shows escalating rates of violence in Colombia during the period 2002-2010 (INMLCF, 2009; CNP, 2010). Homicide and other acts of aggression have increased and expanded from capital cities to smaller urban centers that used to escape the physical violence of the armed conflict (CNP, 2010).

Following the CNP (2010) offenses such as robbery, sexual assault, domestic violence, and crime against natural resources decreased slightly between 2003 and 2004, and increased substantially from 2004 to 2010. According to Handicap International (in CNP, 2010), Colombia during this period became the country with the most victims of anti-personnel mines in the world. Furthermore, the United Nations Office of the High Commissioner for Human Rights in Colombia (UNOHCHR) reported alarming impunity regarding the cases of members of the armed forces involved in murders of hundreds or possibly thousands of civilians that they made appear as 'terrorists fallen in combat' in order to show 'positive results' to their superiors in the frame of the security policy[5] (UNOHCHR, 2006; 2009).

According to the annual report *Forensis* (INMLCF, 2009), 29,433 people died violently in 2009, a 10 percent increase compared to 2008. In 2009, homicides increased by 16.2 percent and violent deaths with undetermined causes increased by 19.4 percent in 2009 compared to 2008.

In 2009, violent episodes substantially increased in capital cities such as Medellín, Cali and Bogotá and smaller urban centers such as Itagüí, Tumaco and Caucasia (INMLCF, 2009). The number of 'non-fatal' violent episodes reported is also higher: 303,471 amongst domestic violence, sexual abuses and accidents (El Tiempo, 2010a). 1,523 women were murdered in 2009 (284 more cases than in 2008). There is evidence of a growing tendency in the use of violence at all levels in society (La Noticia, 2010).

While the murder of unionists and indigenous people decreased substantially from 2002 to 2005, it started to increase continuously again since 2007 (CNP, 2010). In 2011, Colombian analysts have pointed out the widespread use of violent means in society; they are calling attention to a growing culture of intolerance amongst all people. *Semana* magazine published an article titled "Intolerance" posing the question: "Colombians increasingly solve their daily conflicts by using guns and knives, what is going on?" (Semana, 2011a).

> *No se trata de una sensación. Las cifras son dramáticas. Hace siete años, un 10 por ciento de los homicidios registrados por el Observatorio del Delito de la Dijín de la Policía eran atribuidos a riñas; hoy son casi el 40 por ciento del total. En un lustro, entre 2004 y 2009, la tasa de lesiones por violencia, que*

[5] This series of murders has been called 'el escándalo de los falsos positivos' (the scandal of the false positives) (BBC News, 2009; Semana, 2009).

> *compila Medicina Legal, pasó de 200 a más de 300 por 100.000 habitantes. Nueve de cada diez lesiones personales el año pasado fueron por riñas (en 2003, eran seis de cada diez) y los casos de homicidios por "intolerancia social" -una categoría introducida por el Observatorio del Delito de la Dijín hace unos años- vienen subiendo geométricamente desde 2007. Crecen la violencia entre parejas y entre familiares, el maltrato infantil y contra adultos mayores: entre 2004 y 2009, los casos de violencia intrafamiliar saltaron de 60.000, una cifra ya muy elevada, a cerca de 95.000.*[6] (Semana, 2011a)

The security discourse understands *national peace* as a future consequence of the elimination of the 'bad Colombians' via military operations. Under this perspective, the idea of radical respect for human dignity and the right to life are not inalienable anymore. There are clear exceptions to the norm. Under the security policy, human life is not *respected* but barely *tolerated* if the 'other' keeps enough distance.

The security approach to peace that necessarily separates societies into 'good' and 'bad' people uses categories that are blind to systemic conflict analysis and rather understand that those 'bad people' (never oneself) were born as fundamentally evil humans. This is how *peace* in the context of security discourses in Colombia influences arrogant attitudes towards the other: holding an idea of superiority and establishing conditions to *deserve* being treated with dignity.

The argument supporting my research problem is that the notion of peace used by the security policy in Colombia creates cultural separation, gives a very low value to human life and justifies the use of state and private violence in the search for peace and justice. As such it needs to be analyzed by jurists as well as peace and conflict researchers given that ideas of peace out of security inform rights discourses and public policy.

The use of the expressions *tolerance* and *intolerance* in media are interestingly connected to the concepts positive and negative peace that will be dis-

---

[6] It is not mere perception; the figures are dramatic. Seven years ago the Crime Observatory of the National Police (Dijín) reported that 10 percent of the murders were attributed to street fights; today they constitute nearly 40 percent of the total. In five years, between 2004 and 2009, the rate of injuries due to violence compiled by Medicina Legal went from 200 to over 300 per 100,000 inhabitants. Nine out of ten cases of personal injury last year were caused by fights (in 2003 there were six out of ten). The number of cases of killings due to "social intolerance"—a new category introduced by the Crime Observatory— has risen exponentially since 2007. Violence between couples and amongst family members is also on the rise, along with child abuse and violence against elderly people. Between 2004 and 2009, cases of domestic violence jumped from 60,000 —already very high figure— to about 95,000 (Semana, 2011a). Translation by the author.

cussed later in this book. In relation to violence for intolerance, Dietrich proposes a differentiation between tolerance and respect:

> *Respect* contains the insight that recognising the otherness of others must be one's own principle for peace and human dignity. Although the others are treated like members of one's own kinship, there is no intention to adapt them to one's own standards, nor are they simply tolerated as the losers in a strange world. In this way of thinking, respect instead of tolerance or assimilation is a constituent element of peace and human dignity, from where we can derive human rights as one among many possible expressions of this dignity. Conversely, *tolerance* and assimilation are the first steps towards open conflict.
>
> *Tolerance* may help to avoid the extinction of the others, but it includes the prejudice of the superiority of one's own beliefs over the truths of the others. Thus it contains a substantial, geographical and chronosophical limit of recognition. And the violence of purification and ethnic cleansing is already conceivable beyond these limits. (Dietrich, 2000: 14; my emphasis)

As pointed out earlier, legal theory sustains that the main aim of using law is the achievement of 'social peace'. In legal contexts, the adjective 'social' is placed next to the noun 'peace' with a concrete intention: to leave other understandings of peace out of its scope of interest. For instance, *inner* perspectives of peace are generally excluded by jurists in their acts of interpretation and argumentation of rights. As Barraca Mairal asserts:

> *La paz es a la vez un valor, un fin y un bien para el derecho. La paz constituye un valor en el que el derecho hace participar a la convivencia social, por medio de la justicia [...]. La paz que interesa específicamente al derecho es la paz social, la paz de la sociedad humana en cuanto comunidad (y no por ejemplo la paz interior personal o la paz de la conciencia).*[7] (Barraca Mairal, 2005: 133)

This one quotation describes the aim of law in the way I was educated in university: a *national*, *homogenous* idea of peace described and enforced by the law. Subsequently, concrete understandings of peace, the more personal and relational forms of experiencing peace, are not of importance for legal practitioners. In this sense, my query is, are there legal options to respect diverse perspectives of peace in Colombia?

Within the context of armed conflict and current militarization efforts to fight non-state armed groups, military service has become clearly synonymous with being willing to kill and die for 'the nation' (Anderson, 2006) and

---

[7] Peace is at the same time a value, an end, and an asset to law. Peace is a value in which law engages in the issues of social coexistence through justice. The peace that law is specifically interested in is the social peace, the peace of human society as a community (and not the personal inner peace or peace of conscience). Translated by the author.

the Colombian Army is facing an increasing number of conscientious objections from young people (War Resisters' International, 2009).

Following the cultural perspective on peace offered by Dietrich and others (2011), the concept of *peace* is dependent on the context within which it is used. An understanding of peace cannot be reached without the explicit acceptance of its many different notions. Although the dominant paradigm is still the dogmatic application of a universal notion of a single peace, this approach shows to be increasingly ineffectual and inappropriate (Dietrich and others, 2011).

To address the problematic increment of violence and exclusion in the globe under the influence of homogenizing understandings of peace, Dietrich proposed a philosophy of a *plurality of peaces.* He explains that there are at least five main interpretations of the concept of peace across cultures and epochs, namely: the energetic, moral, modern, postmodern, and transrational approaches to peace[8] (Dietrich, 2008). The author proposed the transrational category as a way to integrate all the cultural approaches to peace so that they can respectfully coexist.

According to Dietrich (2006a, 2006b, 2008, 2009), energetic traditions on peace use mainly the spiritual human component to experience harmony, while the moral/modern/postmodern peaces mainly resort to the rational human component to understand and make peace.

Dietrich argues that concepts of *security and justice* also vary according to different understandings on peace. For instance, within the more rational approaches (moral and modern) security and justice are absolute and universal, while in postmodern and transrational understandings they are relative and relational (Dietrich, 2009).

In Colombia, indigenous people are not obliged to perform military service, but every other Colombian male is. The approach to peace of Colombian Indigenous communities diverges strongly from the idea of peace stated in the security policy. It refers more to harmonious relations between opposites than to a social pact that justifies the elimination of enemies. The Colombian Constitutional Court has approached indigenous concepts of peace as the former and consequently has respected their absence from military service. However, non-indigenous people who have expressed genuine energetic

[8] The five interpretations will be developed in detail later.

approaches to peace to argue objections to military service have found their legal claim refused by the Army and Judiciary.[9]

Expressions of diverse interpretations of peace (Dietrich, 2008) can be found within the Colombian population.[10] My hypothesis in this work is that, given the fact that Colombia is constitutionally recognized as pluralistic, multiethnic and multicultural,[11] it should be legally possible to abide by different notions of peace, and not only abide by the one peace that evokes the abstract notion of 'nation' and is enshrined in the security policy.

My concern is to take that pluralism seriously and see what the academic findings of international peace research have to tell jurists about more inclusive and respectful uses of rights; to conceive new possibilities for expressing solidarity (Arendt, 1966) besides joining military efforts. To re-evaluate the meaning of human dignity beyond the bonds of the nation, and following Illich (2006), to rethink peace in a way that facilitates cultures to "blossom in their own, unique ways" (Illich, 2006: 117).

I aim to provide argumentation to support the idea that jurists and litigants can make the national concept of peace *relative* when interpreting and using law, concretely *rights*. As it is argued within the philosophy of the many peaces, peace understood uniquely through an abstract national ideology brings more separation than inclusion to societies.

There are already some tools that can be used in Colombia to widen the legal possibilities for respecting a plurality of peaces via more pluralistic interpretations of rights. These tools include not only a full chapter of civil and political rights (Constitution of Colombia, 1991: Articles 11 to 41), which can be interpreted in a pluralistic manner, but also several legal ac-

---

[9] See jurisprudence of the Clombian Constitutional Court since 1992, examined in Chaper four of this book.

[10] See for instance Julieta Lemaitre Ripoll's elaborations on the diverging meanings of peace and war debated by the Constituent Assembly in 1991 when a new constitutional text was written by representatives of different sectors of the Colombian society. She describes the peace of "the left", the "liberal" and the "conservative" as having different meanings (Lemaitre, 2011).

[11] The articles of the Colombian Political Constitution recognizing the pluralistic, multiethnic and multicultural characters of Colombia are the following: Article 1: "Colombia is a Social State based on the rule of Law, organized as a unitary republic, decentralized, with the autonomy of its territorial units, democratic, participatory and pluralistic, based on respect of human dignity, on the work and solidarity of the individuals who belong to it, and the predominance of the general interest." Article 7: "The State recognizes and protects the ethnic and cultural diversity of the Colombian nation." Article 8: "It is the obligation of the State and of individuals to protect the cultural and natural assets of the nation." Translations available at the University of Richmond's website (Constitution of Colombia, 1991). For the original text in Spanish, see (Constitución Política de Colombia, 1991).

tions that can be used to put those rights into effect. Amongst others, two important actions are: the Tutelage Action[12] and the action of Petition of Unconstitutionality.

In 2009, a group of jurists put together a lawsuit with a petition of unconstitutionality addressed to the Constitutional Court, claiming that the Colombian Conscription Law (Law 48/1993) violated the right to freedom of conscience of conscientious objectors, because it did not include the option to be exempted from military service by the use of conscientious objections. During the process held at the Constitutional Court in 2009 (Decision C-728/09), there was a wide participation of civil society organizations and persons. Numerous intervenors presented written arguments regarding the right to object to military service, claiming perspectives on peace different from the national model based on security.

As a consequence of this case, the Constitutional Court changed its own precedent. The Court adopted a new frame for the interpretation of the right to freedom of conscience that makes it possible to object to military service in Colombia. People could start objecting military service for reasons of conscience since October 2009.

Research Questions

In this research I attempt to answer the following general question: In the case of conscientious objection to military service in Colombia, how does the interpretation of the right to freedom of conscience vary according to Dietrich's families of interpretation of peace, i.e. energetic, moral, modern, postmodern and transrational?

Alongside, I aim to respond to the following specific questions:

- How do different interpretations/perspectives of peace inform legal theory and practice?
- Which perspectives of peace were discussed in the Constitutional case of objections to military service in Colombia (Decision C-728/09)?
- Does the new jurisprudence of decision C-728/09 offer any argumentation of a right to act according to diverse cultural interpretations of peace in Colombia, for instance, energetic, postmodern and transrational inter-

[12] Judicial remedy in Colombia used for protecting fundamental human rights and freedoms.

pretations, in contrast to the duty to act only according to a national interpretation of peace based on security?
- Is there integration of contractual and energetic peaces in the decision adopted by the Constitutional Court regarding objections to the military service in Colombia (Decision C-728/09)?

Method

In order to answer the research questions I will use qualitative interdisciplinary analysis. I intend to review and connect literature from two major disciplines: Peace Studies and Legal Studies, and examine if and how they inform each other. In addition, I will examine a 2009 ruling from the Colombian Constitutional Court on the topic of objections to the military service for reasons of conscience (Decision C-728/09).

With reference to Peace Studies, in *chapter one* I will review contemporary research on the philosophy of many peaces (Dietrich, 2008, 2012) and postmodern philosophy on a more general basis, in resonance to the model of structural and cultural violence proposed by Galtung (1990, 1996). From this review, I intend to gain some insights on what are the cultural variations of peace, what analytical approaches to peace there are and what are the relations and contradictions between them. Based upon this review, I aim to elaborate on the relevance of the pluralistic approach to peace for conflict transformation. The pluralistic approach to peace will serve as theoretical framework for the legal analysis in the following chapters.

As to Legal Studies, in *chapter two* I will review diverse literature on legal philosophy to compile definitions of law and its role in society. With this examination, I will particularly try to discern the importance of the concept *peace* in the creation and functioning of legal institutions. My principal methodology will be to use an open range of perspectives including classic and critical literature.

In *chapter three,* I will make the abstract legal analysis more concrete by addressing the problematic of human rights' norms. I will examine how the argumentation of human dignity and fundamental rights varies according to the underlying concept of peace used by the interpreter. Supported by critical peace studies literature, I will argue that the Colombian security policy — enforced by the law— enhances practices of dehumanization and normalizes violation of rights, causing escalation of violence in Colombia.

Finally, I discuss and aim to demonstrate that peace is a transversal matter to the law. Within this frame, I will study decisions C-728/09 and T-113/09 from the Colombian Constitutional Court; they condense the Constitutional case of conscientious objections to military service in Colombia. The decisions refer to diverse —and many times contradictory— interests regarding the (abstract) national peace and (concrete) alternative peaces of many draftees and their families, including indigenous communities.

For this case study, I read, using the lenses of the *many peaces philosophy,* the diverse arguments brought by jurists, state representatives, and organizations of the civil society to the Colombian Constitutional Court. I want to examine whether those families of legal argumentation could be grouped according to Dietrich's five families of peace. In other words, I want to examine whether the intervenors to the court case expressed plural interpretations of peace and, if so, how those plural perspectives influenced diverse interpretations of the right to object military service for reasons of consciousness. By this methodology I aim to examine how legal studies and practices —specifically human rights law— and peace studies inform each other.

Literature Review

Peace Studies

Stepping out of the abstract national understanding of peace that excludes concrete cultural variations implies a shift in one's philosophical perspective and attitude towards the world. This epistemological move from 'the' truth (one/universal) to a plurality of equally valid truths is to be analyzed before trying to adapt the concept to legal studies. These two epistemological approaches can correspond to the conceptual labels of modernity and postmodernity.

For the analysis of the modern and postmodern perspectives I refer to Lyotard's *Postmodern Condition* (1984) and Deleuze and Guattari's *Thousand Plateaus* (2004). I gathered literature on peace research elaborated upon the basis of postmodern thought, such as Dietrich & Sützl (2006) and Dietrich (2006a, 2008, 2012) who elaborate on the variations of peace, i.e. the diverse interpretations of peace in time and culture; Illich (1982, 2006) on the connections between plural peace and plural development; Koppensteiner (2009) on the postmodern and transpersonal aspects of peace, Muñoz (2006) on the need to embrace imperfect plural peaces; and Vattimo (2006) on the insight of "weak thinking" that peace research uses in connection to Muñoz "imperfect peaces" to support more respectful understandings of peace across cultures.

Dietrich (2008) proposes to perceive *peace* more as an *attitude* than as a status. Accordingly, he refers to the impossibility of addressing it by the use of mere rational means since it involves essential emotional and spiritual human components. In this vein he develops the 'transrational' approach to peace research. In order to grasp the importance of transrationality for conflict transformation, I will take Dietrich's (2006b, 2009) *Call for Transrational Peaces* as main source. Alongside I will use literature on transpersonal psychology and transpersonal transformation such as Maslow (1943, 1971, 1999) and Koppensteiner (2009).

Law

To look at various definitions and classic perspectives on law I will use Suárez (2002) and Nino's (1980a) texts on introduction to law. They bring clear, succinct accounts on Iusnaturalism and Iuspositivism.

Aiming to connect the fields of law and peace studies I will referred to schools of law that elaborate on the inter-relation between law, politics and cultures. These schools take clear position against classic ideas of 'objective,' 'independent' legal norms detached from politics and social values. For this purpose, I used the work of Brian Tamanaha (2004) and Duncan Kennedy (1990, 2002) as main sources. They both are US American scholars dedicated to the study of legal sociology. Kennedy belongs to the Critical Legal Studies (CLS) School developed mainly in the USA and Scandinavia, well known for deconstructing hierarchical power structures served by the law and calling for pluralist argumentations of rights. Tamanaha offers bright contemporary perspectives on the functions of law in society.

From Tamanaha I will particularly use the deconstruction of universalist rights' discourses and his idea of Law's function against tyranny. From Kennedy I will apply the idea of law as model for modern hierarchical education to argue how the legal type of peace excludes cultural variations that diverge from the *national* account. Atienza's idea of 'law as argumentation' (1999) will also help me connect the many peaces with plural argumentation of rights.

Nation-State Peace as Source of Violence

I aim to connect the legal/national understanding of peace based on security with the configuration of cultures of violence in Colombia. Since the Security policy gravitates around the concept 'enemy' I will use Erik Erikson's (1995) concept of *pseudo-speciation* (in Friedman, 2000; Hoover, 2004) to elaborate on how thousands of Colombians categorized as 'enemies' by the security policy are officially considered less than human. I argue that when their death is not called *homicide* anymore, we are facing what Arendt called the loss of the 'right to have rights'. I will use Arendt's *Origins of Totalitarism* (1966) to expand on some violent structures involved in contractual peaces. I will also invoke Judith Butler's (2006) reference to the precarious life of dehumanized humans to elaborate on the poor consideration of human dignity in the security policy in Colombia.

My arguments will be further sustained by the works of Maslow (1943), Zimbardo (2008) and Rosenberg (2003) in the field of psychology. Philip Zimbardo goes beyond the legal account on human aggression, which he calls "dark side," offering a more empathetic perspective. He approaches aggression as a human response to surviving violent systems. Zimbardo argues that all humans have potential for good and evil and that social systems of rejection, repression and radical identification of people according to their expected roles enhance aggressive responses. I will also use Rosenberg's understanding of violence partly as an "expression of unmet human needs" (2003) and Maslow's pyramid of human needs (1943) to support the idea that conflict policymaking based on a nation-state-like interpretation of peace radicalizes the enemy identity and therefore constitutes structural and cultural violence (Galtung, 1990, 1996).

Both Zimbardo and Rosenberg are US American scholars whose works challenge the understanding of human aggression only as individual guilt, and elaborate on psychological responses to structures. Zimbardo grew up around crime in an unprivileged area in New York City. Rosenberg has a Jewish background also marked for stigmatization. They developed systemic approaches in which 'evil' is not an essential identity of the individual but part of social systems in which we all participate via language, norms, science, religion, ideology and other cultural means. Good and evil exist in human behavior as part of a whole and we create cultures that foster more one or the other in different times. I will use this systemic perspective in connection with Dietrich's Transrational Peaces to challenge the concept of human dignity in the Colombian security policy and problematize the nation-state-like interpretation of peace that seeks the extermination of 'enemies'.

Along with Echavarría's understanding of radical political identities in the frame of the Colombian security policy (2010), I will use Zimbardo and Rosenberg's views to connect the radical roles of 'good' and 'evil' persons with the instrumentalisation of the legal value of *solidarity*. I will argue that the use of *solidarity* in Colombian jurisprudence on military service was used until 2009 merely to enhance aggressive responses to conflict in the Colombian people and to reinforce radical political identities.

Structure

To address the aforementioned problem and answer the proposed research questions, I will develop an academic analysis in four main chapters.

(1) The first chapter comprises a study of contemporary peace research looking specifically at the theory of the many peaces and transrational approaches to peace. It will serve as a conceptual framework for the legal analysis and the case study.

(2) The second chapter refers to the law, its function in society and the role of the concept 'peace' in Legal Studies.

(3) The third chapter is a transition from the general theory of law to Human Rights law. It revises the concept of 'human dignity' and rights discourses from peace studies perspectives, specifically from the theory of the many peaces.

(4) The fourth and last chapter contains the case study. It consists of an analysis of the Colombian conscription system and its relation to notions of national solidarity and national peace out of security. In this chapter, I will analyze the legal case of conscientious objections to military service held in ruling C-728/09 of the Colombian Constitutional Court, looking at how the argumentation of rights varies according to different perspectives on peace held by the interpreter.

In the last chapter, my concluding remarks will bring together the main reflections upon which I elaborate in this text: the plurality of peaces framework, the legal theory and practices, and the right to abide by different notions of peace in Colombia. I will identify the connecting points and contradictions amongst these fields and draw some lessons gained from this research process.

1. CONCEPTUAL FRAMEWORK: PLURALITY OF PEACES

Conceptualizing the 'one world peace' is in itself intellectual violence, because it lacks respect for otherness and its secrets. (Dietrich & Sützl, 2006)

INTRODUCTION

In relation to the case of conscientious objection to military service in Colombia, I have proposed the query how does the interpretation of the right to freedom of conscience vary according to Dietrich's five cultural variations of peace, i.e. energetic, moral, modern, postmodern and transrational? In this chapter, I will approach the question by studying the philosophy of the 'plurality of peaces' and the five families of interpretation of peace in culture and time (Dietrich, 2008).

I aim to clarify what modernity, postmodernity and transrationality are, and how these philosophical perspectives influence different —even contradictory— understandings of peace and conflict. In addition, I want to expose the content of the five cultural variations of peace described by Dietrich (2008) explaining how pluralistic approaches to peace come to be considered more appropriate for the facilitation of cultures of sustainable non-violence, or what Boulding (2000) calls "cultures of peace."

This theoretical framework will be crucial for the forthcoming analysis of the role of peace in legal theory and practice, and for elucidating to which of the variations of peace the legal type of peace refers. It will also allow me to analyze the concepts of peace used in the jurisprudence on objections to military service in Colombia and elaborate on the link between the *one/national* peace and the escalation of cultural violence (Galtung, 1990) experienced since 2008 in the country (INMLCF, 2009)

1.1 PRELIMINARY CONCEPTS

Before entering the study of the five families of interpretation of peace in culture (Dietrich, 2008, 2012), I will introduce the concepts of *positive and negative peace* and the *three dimensions of violence* described by Johan Galtung (1990, 1996). These are analytical tools of peace research that will enrich the lecture of the theory of the many peaces, the role of peace in legal theory and practice, and the case study on objections to military service in Colombia.

1.1.1 Positive and Negative Peace

Johan Galtung (1996) suggested that the word 'peace' sometimes indicates the *absence* and other times the *presence* of certain social conditions. On the one hand, peace refers to the *absence* of violence; on the other hand, peace refers to the presence of harmony and joy. In the case of the former, there is 'peace' when there is no open direct aggression.

Considering that here peace is not defined by what it is but by 'what it is not', Galtung categorizes it as *negative peace*. This perspective involves the suppression of aggressive energy in societies by threatening people with jail, the death penalty, and many other forms of social exclusion in case they resort to violence.

Efforts to achieve negative peace emphasize managing interpersonal and organizational conflict in order to *control, contain, and reduce* actual and potential violence. Political or physical elimination of the enemy, ceasefires, and signature of peace agreements are examples of negative peace in cases of organizational conflict. Stop talking to someone altogether is an example in cases of interpersonal conflict.

Beyond the forced absence of aggression peace also indicates *presence* of conditions for a fully expressed human life in harmony, which Galtung (1996) calls *positive peace*. Galtung sees the presence of *positive peace* in actual actions or happenings such as kindness and good to the body, mind and spirit of the self and others; in freedom of expression, dialogue, integration, participation and solidarity; and in legitimation of cultures of peace via religion, ideology, language, art, science, and media. The underlying idea in the concept of positive peace is an *opening* for human potentials and capabilities instead of repressing them (Galtung, 1996: 32).

Rosenberg (2003) explains that we humans resort to violence to express frustration for our unmet physical and emotional needs. According to his analyses, apart from our physical sphere of needs, we all have emotional needs to be appreciated, included, respected and acknowledged; we need our life and suffering to be honoured.[13] Following Rosenberg's systemic understanding of aggression, Galtung's negative peace involves the suppression of those expressions of frustration while positive peace involves acknowledging and actively dealing with unmet needs that lead to frustration and consequently to aggression.

1.1.2 Dimensions of Violence

Galtung (1990) comments that destructive and alienating situations in societies do not come only from the use of direct physical violence, but from three different dimensions of violence: direct, structural, and cultural. The last two cyclically cause direct violence and are especially difficult to acknowledge and resist (Zimbardo, 2008).

According to Galtung, *direct violence* refers to verbal or physical aggression harming the body, mind, or spirit of others or the self; *structural violence* refers to political-repressive and economic-exploitative violence supported by structural segmentation/marginalization; and *cultural violence* refers to aspects of culture —not entire cultures— exemplified by religion and ideology, language and art, empirical science and formal science, that can be used to justify or legitimize direct or structural violence via, for instance, stereotypes, myths, and beliefs that fuel discrimination (Galtung, 1990).[14]

1.2 The *One* Peace: Modernity

In the context of a national idea of peace based on security, in September 2010, the Colombian Minister of Defense Rodrigo Rivera referred publicly to the military strategy chosen by the Government at the time to deal with non-state armed groups, especially the guerrilla group called Revolutionary Armed Forces of Colombia-Popular Army (FARC-EP), he said: "*hago el llamado para que se desmovilicen* [*las* FARC] *porque vamos a conquistar la*

---

[13] For further analysis on systemic approaches to conflict, see for instance Hellinger (2002, 2003) and Cohen (2009).

[14] Later I will use the structural and cultural dimensions of violence to frame the analysis of the security policy's interpretation of peace and challenge the resulting homogenizing argumentation of rights in jurisprudence on military service in Colombia.

paz, con la razón o con la fuerza. Nuestras fuerzas militares mantendrán la ofensiva, [...] seguiremos arreciando contra las Farc"[15] (El Espectador, 2010).[16]

This statement involves the understanding that all Colombians share the same (national) idea of peace based on the exclusion or extermination of members of the Colombian society that resort to the use of violent means. It uses one interpretation of peace as universal or homogeneous.

The understanding of peace as a *universal* concept does not appear in Colombia and other countries as unlinked from other social phenomena. It exists in a global context of a "concrete societal project characterized by Newtonian physics, Cartesian reductionism, the nation-state of Thomas Hobbes, and the capitalist world system" (Dietrich & Sützl, 2006: 283). It derives from Socrates' and Plato's conceptualizations of the *one truth*, and belongs to a human manner of understanding and relating to the universe defined by scholars as *Modernity*.

Esteva and Prakash (1998: 9) refer to three main characteristics of modernity in what they call *modern sacred cows* defined as *certainties* or moral ideas which cannot be questioned by modern minds: (1) *The myth of global thinking*, intellectual counterpart of the global economy, the idea —entrenched in globalization— that there is only one, universally valid way of understanding social reality; (2) *Universality of human rights*, based in Western-defined notions despite differences in traditions, faith and moral outlook, and (3) *The myth of the individual self* as opposed to people in-community. These certainties are the object of deconstruction by postmodern thinkers.

Following Jean-François Lyotard, modernism is based upon *metanarratives* (Lyotard, 1984: 27), which legitimate further scientific knowledge but are not open to rational argumentation themselves. According to Koppensteiner (2009), Lyotard shows how this concern with legitimation via first principles arises with Plato and his cave allegory[17] and continually resurfaces

[15] Acronym for Fuerzas Armadas Revolucionarias de Colombia or the Revolutionary Armed Forces of Colombia.

[16] "I call on them [guerrilla group FARC] to demobilize, because we will conquer peace, either by the use of reason or by the use of force. Our military forces remain on the offensive (...) we will continue raging against the FARC" (El Espectador, 2010). Translation by the author.

[17] In the cave allegory, Plato imagines a group of people who have been held prisoner in a cave deep inside a mountain all of their lives, so that the cave is the only place they know. They face a blank wall and watch shadows projected on it by things passing in front of a fire behind them, and begin to ascribe forms to these shadows. According to Plato, the shadows are as close as the prisoners get to seeing reality. He then explains how the philosopher is like a

as, for example, in Descartes' *Discourse on Method.* It is a story or (meta)narrative because on its own premises it can neither be proven nor refuted (Koppensteiner, 2009: 15).

The idea of the one unquestionable truth as the highest principle of thinking since the Plato's cave allegory takes Mediterranean cultures into giving more and more importance to *reason.* Reason is the means by which they are able to find the one truth. Wilber refers to modernity as *the Enlightenment paradigm* (Wilber, 2007: 86). This process of human focusing on explicable, logical phenomena and their ability to explain it evolved, on the one hand, into the magnificent development of natural sciences via Newtonian physics and the human possibility of understanding natural laws in order to predict and control phenomena. Achievements in science have brought and keep bringing us enormous benefits in terms of human comfort and possibilities to live and relate to the universe in many ways.

On the other hand, modernity has brought a new set of principles derived from the rightness of the one truth, because it implies also considering that some things are not truth, resulting in humans asking themselves what do with those non-truths and, how to relate to them. One possibility is to try to cut out their existence; hence, a new need is born: a need for the *elimination of wrongness.* In this vein peace theorists have suggested that the attempts of persons and cultures to achieve peace in the way they understand it and trying to expand that achievement universally is the base of much of the violence experienced by humans.

Dietrich and Sützl (2006) explain that International Peace Research as an academic discipline was born at the beginning of the twentieth century out of the painful violence of World War I. It was in 1919 when the British and US American delegations at the Paris Peace Conference decided to establish academic institutions for research on international relations with the aim of finding out how to fix violence in the globe, but what followed was World War II and later the "shocking insight that this century did not bring a system of one/universal peace, but an escalation of violence and destruction unprecedented in human history" (Dietrich & Sützl, 2006: 292).

---

prisoner who is freed from the cave and comes to understand that the shadows on the wall are not constitutive of reality at all, but an imaginary world made by the illusion of what our senses perceive. For Plato, the philosopher is the one who can perceive the true form of reality rather than the mere shadows as those seen by the prisoners in the cave. For further analysis see Heidegger & Sadler (2002).

> [Peace research] institutions were to conduct their research for several decades and through another World War before it became acceptable among experts to suspect that it may be precisely this linear, universalist and reductionist basic assumption aimed at a paradise on earth, the one truth, the one and perpetual peace, the one world society, and the one civilising process that carries in it the germ of a self-reproductive structure of violence, and that this kind of idea of salvation is in itself intellectual violence because it simply lacks respect for otherness and its secrets. How is one to treat others like members of one's own kin if the difference among kins has long been eliminated through nationalisation and universalisation, and as long as the other is still considered synonymous with imperfection? (Dietrich & Sützl, 2006: 292)

The universalism of modernity brings along the separation of beings and behaviors according to dual categories derived from the idea of truth, like correct/incorrect, normal/abnormal, good/evil, among others, which have culturally boiled in forms of social exclusion, discrimination, absolutist regimes and misery for those who do not fit into the accepted category, whatever it may be. Following Dietrich & Sützl (2006), there are at least two options for interpreting this state: from a *pessimistic* point of view, such a state could be interpreted and experienced as loss of values and orientation known as *anomy* (condition of fear and lack of orientation of individuals, lack of regulation in and among societies) and if one adopts an *optimistic* perspective, then arises the insight that the absence of the one truth allows for a democratic plurality of truths.

1.3 The Many Peaces: Postmodernity

Ivan Illich asserts that under the cover of development and the attempt to achieve the one truth of progress, "a worldwide war has been waged against people's peace" (Illich, 2006: 173). He points at culture as the source for the meaning to peace. "Each ethnos —people, community and culture has been mirrored, symbolically expressed and reinforced by its own ethos— myth, law, goddess, ideal of peace. Peace is as vernacular as speech" (Illich, 2006: 173). For instance "Jewish Shalom and Roman Pax had nothing to do with each other" (2006: 174). In the same vein, Dietrich and Sützl said farewell to the one peace of modernity:

> The world [...] needs more than one peace for concrete societies and communities to be able to organize themselves. The peaces do not become mutually compatible the moment everybody understands one another, but when all live in their own peace, that is, treat others like the members of their own kin, and so respect them even if they do not understand them. Let us look for our place

> and act in accordance with it! Let us talk about the many peaces. (Dietrich & Sützl, 2006: 301)

Such understanding of peace as contextual, concrete, vernacular and therefore plural is what characterizes the philosophy of the many peaces. This way of understanding peace is a consequence of a critical shared state of mind that refers to disillusionment of absolute truths. A state of mind called *postmodernity.*

1.3.1 European Postmodernity

Postmodernism is a theoretical worldview or academic discipline born in Europe in the second half of the nineteenth century whose roots are placed in the disappointment in modernism. Koppensteiner (2009) explains that postmodernism is a line of skeptical thinking towards modernity, at the beginning of which stands the work of Friedrich Nietzsche followed up by many authors critically engaged with the project of modernity such as Martin Heidegger, Wolfgang Schirmacher, Gianni Vattimo, Jean François Lyotard, Jacques Derrida, Gilles Deleuze, Felix Guattari, Michael Foucault and Jean Baudrillard (Koppensteiner, 2009: 14).

Postmodernism is a critical reaction to the upheaval of the twentieth century (Koppensteiner, 2010). It is a stream of thought that by the use of rational means criticizes modern absolute rationalism and calls for *pluralistic relativism.* Wilber understands postmodernism as a "worldview characterized by antihierarchy, social construction of reality, strong equality, multiculturalism and relativistic value systems" (Wilber, 2000: 50).

Postmodernity does not offer a new truth to replace 'the' modern truth but simply refers to that disillusioning phase of the same modernity in which people increasingly doubt the universalism of this paradigm. It stands for the recognition of many possible truths, for the celebration of diversity and relative contextual understandings of the world. It criticizes absolute approaches where *abnormal/incorrect* elements are rejected and excluded from social systems; this is why postmodernism is closely related to cultural studies. Dietrich & Sützl (2006: 283) observe that "people have become aware of the relativity of those truths in whose absolute validity they used to believe. As a consequence, those truths have lost their binding character."

Postmodernism and postmodern peace researchers call for diversity. It is precisely in this context where "A Call for Many Peaces" was written initially as a working paper in 1997 (Dietrich & Sützl, 1997) and later on published as part of the book *Key Texts for Peace Studies* (Dietrich & Sützl, 2006).[18] The authors suggest the understanding of peace as a *noun in plural* after arguing that the concept of *one/universal* peace is a violent discriminating project of modernity.

1.3.2 Postmodernism's Key Contributions to Peace Studies

Some of the key postmodern contributions used by peace researchers to suggest the conceptualization of peace as a plural, imperfect process are amongst others Vattimo's idea of *weak thinking* (Vattimo, 2006), Gödel's *Incompleteness Theorems* (Drucker, 2008), Deleuze and Guattari's (2004) *Rhizome* and Francisco Munoz's (2006) concept of *Imperfect Peace*. They all provide arguments on how the one truth of modernity could be understood as *relative* instead of absolute. In the following section I will briefly explore the contents of these contributions.

Weak thinking

Gianni Vattimo's concept of *weak thinking* (2006) refers to the possibility of permanently transforming what one has learnt and taken for granted, to the ability to go beyond strong metaphysics, not by rejecting them but rather by embracing and distorting them. Weak thinking is explained by Koppensteiner (2009:19) as a "form of thinking which is aware of its own situatedness and contingency, and takes into account the historical background against which and within which it is formed." Opposed to forms of *strong thinking*, this concept approaches relative truths and opens spaces in peace research for the understanding of peace as an experience, which is different in every culture and person, and also transforms over the course of a person's life.

Incompleteness Theorems

Gödel's two Incompleteness Theorems presented in his doctoral thesis published in 1931 are considered important both in mathematical logic and in the philosophy of mathematics, and they are now also considered valuable in

---

[18] Published under the German title *Schlüsseltexte der Friedensforschung*.

peace research (Dietrich, 2008, 2012). They basically refer to the "unprovability of consistency" (Drucker, 2008: 87), which stipulates that

> [A] sufficiently powerful formal system has to be either incomplete or contradictory. It can be consistent or complete, but never both at the same time. If a system is in itself completely consistent, then there are fundamental truths that cannot be derived from it. That is why it is incomplete. But if the system is changed in such manner that it can take in those truths, that is, if completeness is striven for, then contradictions will appear in some places and it will be inconsistent. (Dietrich, 2012: 261)

Gödel's theorems, in combination with the discussions in which he was involved with other mathematicians and philosophers of the time, demonstrated what Drucker calls "Gödel's awareness of the formal undefinability of the notion of truth" (Drucker, 2008: 88). Gödel's theorems are recognized to escape the known *references of self-reference* used to denote a statement that refers to itself or is its own referent. The philosophical interest in self-reference is to a large extent centered on paradoxes, or descriptions of reality which appear contradictory but still belong together (Stanford Encyclopedia of Philosophy, 2008).

Rhizomes

On their part, Deleuze and Guattari's concept of rhizome (2004) applied to social sciences was first published in 1987 and comes from botany. In natural sciences the word rhizome describes a horizontal, underground plant stem capable of producing the shoot and root systems of a new plant. This capability allows the parent plant to propagate vegetatively and enables a plant to survive an annual unfavorable season underground (Encyclopedia Britannica, 2010). Examples of rhizomes are bamboos, ginger and couch grass; Deleuze and Guattari (2004: 10) also refer to ants as animal rhizomes. They contrast rhizomes with the arborecent unit (the one), explaining that while trees or roots have individual-hierarchical structures, rhizomes (the multiple) are horizontal nets that allow immediate connections between any of its points. Rhizomes are used as a concept in philosophy in an attempt to apprehend multiplicities in contrast to hierarchical structures of inclusion and exclusion.

Deleuze and Guattari affirm that "there are no points or positions in a rhizome such as those found in a structure, tree or root" thus "the notion of unity appears only when there is a power takeover in the multiplicity by the signifier" (Deleuze and Guattari 2004: 10). The authors describe four main principles of rhizomes: (1) *connection and heterogeneity*: any point of a rhizome system can be connected to anything other and must be, (2) *multiplicity*: as in contrast to individuality or binary models, (3) *asignifying rupture*: a rhizome may be broken but it will start up again, and (4) *cartography and decalcomania*: differing from any idea of genetic axis or deep structure, rhizomes are more like a map than like a tracing, which always comes back to the same point and is always a copy; rhizomes rather foster connections between fields, are open, and connectable (Deleuze & Guattari, 2004: 7-14).

The meaning given to rhizomes in the context of postmodernity is important for peace studies as regarding the understanding of relationality as the basis of the human condition and detaching from the modern concept of *individuum* or the *in-dividual*: the *unit* which cannot be divided. Following Koppensteiner, from postmodern perspectives "the subject in this rendering is no longer *indivisible* and neither is it a single unit *separable from its surroundings*" (Koppensteiner, 2009: 118; my emphasis).

Imperfect Peace

Lastly, Francisco Muñoz's concept of *Imperfect Peace* (Muñoz, 2006) contrasts the modern way of understanding peace that refers to the absence of violence, conflict and contradiction (negative peace) and as such implies a certain utopia, state of purity or perfection in the sense of ideal status or finished process. According to Muñoz, a desired state of perfection with no conflict is unattainable; then the modern idea of peace only leads to frustration. Muñoz asserts that modernism uses violent means to achieve this ideal state of purity. He proposes a *conflictive or unfinished understanding of peace,* one in permanent construction, a continuous process beyond the antagonist dualism of the pacifist/violent, good/evil, an understanding of the *fertility* of the many situations in-between those dual categories.

1.3.3 Postmodernity in Latin America

Why use European postmodernity as a theoretical framework in a thesis about legal argumentation in Colombia? My reason to explore postmodernity is its philosophical argumentation of the possibility of many coexistent truths, its deconstruction of universalist ideas of peace, conflict and law, together with its opening for respectful understandings of *otherness*, as an alternative to structural exclusion. Before moving into the study of peaces in Colombian jurisprudence, I will first search for the presence of postmodernism as theoretical worldview in Latin America.

Actually, there is debate about the existence of a Latin American postmodernity as an academic discipline. Postmodernism as an academic search was born and developed by European scholars in the context of the European

Enlightenment. But the debate is not serene. On the one side, authors such as Luis and González (1994: ix-xiv) maintain that there is a postmodern tradition in Latin America and it manifests for instance through the so-called *Boom* period of literature of the 1960s, when novels started to use experimental fiction. Many of those novels included their own criticism and even suggested a form or perspective from which they should be read. Some of them aimed to question the limits between the real and the magic, reality and dreams, the many realities, and to reveal that knowledge is not a given but is subject of interpretation (Luis and González, 1994: ix-xiv).

According to Luis and González, distinguished postmodern novels are *La Muerte de Artemio Cruz* (Fuentes, 1962), *Rayuela* (Cortázar, 1963) *La Casa Verde* (Vargas Llosa, 1968) *Tres Tristes Tigres* (Infante, 1990) and *Cien Años de Soledad* (García Márquez, 1967). These works reflect the local conditions of Mexico, Argentina, Peru, Cuba and Colombia respectively and also proposed theoretical issues appealing to a broader audience. Luis and González further claim that contemporary Latin American Fiction is postmodern:

> Characteristic of this fiction is the decentering of discourse and the political question of dominant ideologies. Such opposition to reigning structures has a long tradition in Latin America and can be traced back to early Amerindian and slave rebellions [...]. Latin American literature and politics are inextricably related and in the postmodern period the decentering discourse is present in literature as well as in politics and history. (Luis & González, 1994: xi)

On the other side of the debate, some authors argue that it is impossible to talk about a Latin American postmodernity when the region has not yet completed the basics of modernity, given that many Latin Americans are actually illiterate (Muñoz, 1998 quoted in Espinoza, 2001). However, such arguments can be challenged when clarifying that postmodernism is not an epoch after modernity, but rather a state of mind (Dietrich & Sützl, 2006: 283). Both in Europe and Latin America there is disillusionment from modernity as homogenizing project. There is disappointment from its exclusive structures that deny diversity and there are also calls for the respect of plurality expressed via critical thinking towards totalizing discourses. What is important to remark is that both *decentering projects* —Latin American and European— come from different stimuli and have different connotations.

> *Estas manifestaciones culturales [postmodernas] han surgido en el subcontinente por diferentes razones y circunstancias a las observadas en las sociedades euro-norteamericanas y, principalmente, son el resultado de una diferente forma de experimentar el modernismo. No es una cuestión de imitar o transcribir un debate sobre la crisis de la modernidad en el mundo europeo,*

> *sino, de pensar acerca de la forma en que Latino América ha experimentado esa modernidad y su crisis, viviéndola en una forma distinta.*[19]

While in Europe postmodernity comes from disillusionment of metanarratives and instrumental reason, in Latin America —Espinoza explains— it rather comes from oppression by hegemonic capitalist cultures which fosters a need for defending the own identity and right to be different (Espinoza, 2001).

According to Larraín 1996: 57) "the reception of postmodernism in Latin America seems to come from the fact that it is the only contemporary theory that allows Latin America to have its own voice and legitimates its right to be different." Larraín comments that the economic failure of many Latin American countries and subsequent military dictatorships led many intellectuals to strongly criticize instrumental reason and to revalue a different type of cultural identity. In this vein, essentialist streams affirm that strong modernizing attempts in Latin America can only fail as long as they do not respect the Latin American identity (Larraín, 1996).

Elaborating on Sunkel (1988) and Parker's (1973) works, Larraín explains how an opposition between two different cultural models starts to become clearer: the European rational-illustrated and the Latin American symbolic-dramatic. The first has a more abstract-conceptual model and believes in instrumental reason. It is reason used as a means for controlling nature and achieving material progress. The second has a more aesthetic-transcendent approach to reality; it emphasizes images, rituals and appeals to sensitivity. It is to the defense of this Latin American identity that postmodernism has contributed specially in the 1980s (Larraín, 1996: 57-58).

To sum up, in Latin America as in Europe where postmodernism was born as an academic discipline, there is disillusionment from modernity as a homogenizing project, the narratives of the one peace and progress have been and are also in crisis in Latin America. The social call for diverse truths is present for instance in Latin American literature, and not least, in court cases, as I aim to show later in this book.

---

[19] These cultural events [postmodern] have emerged in the subcontinent for different reasons and circumstances to those observed in Euro-Northamerican societies and, mainly, are the result of a different way to experience modernity. It is not a question of imitating or transcribing a debate on the crisis of modernity in the European world, but about thinking how Latin America has experienced that modernity and its crisis, by living in a different way. (Fuenzalida & Fuenzalida, 2007). Translation by the author.

1.3.4 Energetic, Moral, Modern and Postmodern Peaces

"Let us look for our place and act in accordance with it! Let us talk about the many peaces" (Dietrich & Sützl, 2006: 301). With this postmodern call for *Many Peaces,* Dietrich elaborated on the differentiation of the possible forms of understanding and experiencing peace in history and culture, proposing a categorization of five main families of interpretation of peace: the energetic, the moral, the modern, the postmodern and the transrational peaces. Such a system of classification is not necessarily chronological neither exhaustive; it is rather a classification according to different understandings of the universe (Dietrich, 2006a). The following session presents a brief account on the different interpretations of peace in time and culture.

Energetic Peace

From this perspective, peace is experienced as *harmony.* It is thought to be a kind of *philosophia perennis*[20] (Koppensteiner, 2010) or a recurring insight independent of specific cultural context or intellectual epoch. The cosmos, nature, society, and persons are seen as being in an inextricable reciprocal relationship, which, when balanced, is experienced as peace. The balance of dualities, represented by the *Yin Yang*, shows how dualities are *complementary* rather than exclusive; they shape the universe into a whole where everything is related to everything else. As such, even the smallest being is important, is related to all others, and is divine. From this perspective, the human being is always relational.

Energetic interpretations of peace can be found in all continents and at all times, yet they are generally linked only to indigenous and native pre-colonial communities in Africa and the Americas as well as in eastern cultures, where being nourished by Mother Nature and participating in the harmonious flux of all visible and invisible things is experienced as peace. It is an ancient concept and is not too far away from what we still know today from Taoism, Hinduism or Buddhism, including mystical traditions of Judaism, Christianity and Islam (Dietrich 2006a: 3). But harmony as embodied and spiritual experience is not necessarily tied to any religion or institution.

---

[20] Concept introduced initially by Aldous Huxley in the 1940s. It assumes that beneath the institutional superstructure all religions are based on a direct mystical experience that is timeless and beyond language (Koppensteiner, 2010).

There are traditions of energetic peaces in Latin America and specifically in Colombia that have a strong presence. Espinoza (2001) explicates that in pre-Columbian cultures, for example, the concepts of development and peace of communities, unlike their modern understanding, were linked amongst other aspects to the experience of the sacred-mystic. To achieve a state of ceremonial and existential attitude used to be of high value for those cultures. Ritualizing of everyday life was very meaningful not only as concerning sublime forms of social conviviality based on mutual respect, but also regarding encouragement of human relations with nature and the universe (Espinoza, 2001). Such energetic traditions are still present in sectors of Colombian communities, not only in closed circles of indigenous peoples but also permeating other cultures in the form of religiosity, spirituality or different forms of ethics.

Moral Peace

Moving away from the energetic approach, peace from moral perspectives starts to be *universal* instead of local, *understood* more than experienced, and based on categorical *norms* more than relations. Peace here is defined as future salvation from the troubles of existence, under the condition that norms are correctly followed. Norms are established by the one, personalized and male God who —now— is separated from humans (Dietrich, 2008, 2012).

This conception of peace begins to take place in the European world when Mediterranean cultures turn towards the philosophy of an *unquestionable* truth. From this philosophy it derived the establishment of absolute norms promoting powerful institutions, so the *social fit* (obedience) becomes a peacemaking imperative for the individual. In this light, Augustine and later Thomas Aquinas derived a reduced right to just war for peace (*bellum lustrum*) from the unavoidability of imperfection in temporary peace and justice on earth, if one of the conflicting parties obviously is at fault (Dietrich 2006a).

Monotheist religions have a strong presence in Colombia. The Catholic Church, concretely, was institutionalized in the Latin American region by Spanish conquerors that battled the worldviews of the natives aiming to 'civilize' them. Hence, ideas of peace referring to a future prize to be given by an outside observer, male God, are one of the cultural variations of peace in Colombia. It coexists with the approach of native cultures that survived and are nowadays protected by the law as an essential part of the country's cultural diversity.

Due to its strong presence, the moral approach is part of public debates in the creation or elimination of laws. The moral is one of the forms to judge legal norms according to absolute ideals of justice/injustice. The former Colombian Constitution (1886) referred to Catholicism as the state-religion, established God as the supreme source of public power and invoked the protection of (the Catholic) God for the well being of the nation (Malagón, 2010). Thence, moral arguments were very common in legal debates until 1991 when the nation was declared secular with the expedition of a new constitutional text.

In 1993 the Constitutional Court referred to the incompatibility between one state-religion and the nation's cultural plurality (Decision C-027/93). Since then, the use of catholic-oriented moral arguments to give absolute meaning to rights was discouraged.

Modern Peace

Modernity understands peace as a contractually arranged absence of direct violence. As explained before, *modernity* is a worldview related to the universality of truth, from which also the moral peace derives its basis. What makes the modern concept different from the moral is the replacement of God (as provider of right norms and consequently peace) with *reason*. Modernity sees the universe as made out of material objects which can be analyzed, understood and improved; it responds to the principles of cause and effect. God is no longer necessary because scientific truth is absolute. The emergence of modern concepts of peace is instigated by the crisis of the moral institution of the Church, the scientific and economic upheavals, the traumatic experiences of war, and the fear and hope they engender in people during the process of the Enlightenment and secularization (Koppensteiner, 2010).

The nation-state appears as the higher manifestation of reason, with promises of security, development and a 'perfect peace' (Muñoz, 2006). By creating and using absolute rules and punishment the nation-state pursues to control the appearance of the *wrong, unjust,* and *immoral* behaviors. Such abstract norms are created in the hope that one day in the future nations will achieve a perfect social order and justice. International law also uses components of peace based on a universal reason.

This is the perspective on peace that has inspired militarization norms in Colombia since 2002. This variation, with strict focus on the rational-logic component, makes it possible to understand peace as a status of homogenization or common obedience of abstract norms. Therefore, relative-concrete situations of peace are left behind the scope of the law: they involve risk, thus *disorder* and *insecurity*.

Postmodern Peace(s)

As mentioned previously, postmodernity is born out of disappointment in modernity. It tells us that modernity has not brought peace as it promised, but escalation of violence. It rejects modern utopias of perfection, security, development and all universalisms, which are considered homogenizing and hence lacking respect for otherness. Postmodern scholars consider attempts to *secure* peace as reproducing violence, thereof arises an acceptance of vulnerability and risk, and the recognition of the human condition as a perpetual process of becoming (Koppensteiner, 2010). Postmodernity refuses absolute values and calls for pluralist relativism and for celebration of diversity beyond ultimate values. It therefore does not offer one concluded concept of peace; postmodern peaces exist in concrete moments and places whenever life flows and becomes.

These concepts have also inspired different manners of giving meaning to conflict. Whereas in modernity, conflict is synonyms with wrongness and as such something to be avoided, to be *resolved* or *fixed,* postmodernity opens up for the inclusion of conflict as a source of creative energy for transformation, as an essential part of life's process of flowing and becoming. Galtung, for instance, differentiates between *conflict* and *violence*, understanding the first as creative energy for social transformation and violence as one of the possible forms to deal with conflict and arguing that peace is "what we have when creative conflict transformation takes place nonviolently" (Galtung, 1996: 265).

Postmodern thought opens up to plurality and relativism. In so doing, it makes room for many persons, groups, elements and ideas, even the ones excluded by modernity, to bring in new possibilities for cultures of respect. However, being in postmodernity is an entirely *rational* project of deconstruction, as pointed out by Wilber, it is also trapped in the limits of the explicability of things by modern means with which it continues to be a state of mind and continues to lead to anomy. "It [postmodernity] says: *there are no universal truths*, but that stance itself claims to be universally true" (Wilber, 2007: 92).

A guiding question regarding the *limitations of reason* emerges in postmodern discourse. Postmodernity, therefore, realizes the loss of *harmony* since the conceptualization of 'the' *truth* but does not have the tools to bring it back. According to Dietrich, "this is the fundamental dilemma of postmodern thinking as a tool of Peace Research" (2006b: 12) and starting point of his argumentation on the *transrational* understandings of peace.

Colombian law had an important turn into postmodernism with the promulgation of the 1991 Constitution "that emphasized regionalization, ideological pluralism and multiculturalism" (Botero, 2006: 46). In this context, the rights of oppressed communities started to gain importance and jurists started to use balancing exercises amongst conflicting interests. The right to equality turned into a right to *being different*[21] and a whole new way of arguing fundamental rights started to take place at the core of the Constitutional Court.

1.4 *Transrational* Peaces

Dietrich explains that "Galtung tried to redefine peace as the ability to transform conflicts by empathy, non-violence and creativity. Hence he crosses the Rubicon of postmodernity when he understands peace as an *attitude*, rather close to Gandhi's definition of *ahimsa*, and not as a *status* anymore" (Dietrich, 2000: 13).

The concept of Transrational Peaces is a new approach in contemporary peace research that considers both the rational and the spiritual spheres of human perception to be fundamental for the understanding of peace. Aiming at this type of understanding, Dietrich addresses the postmodern dilemma by asserting that when enriched with some orientative knowledge, not all truths of modernity have to be rejected to be able to respect the parallel existence of truths; they may be incompatible with modernity but not necessarily in conflict with it.

Wilber suggests the same idea mentioning that modernity is not wrong but rather too narrow and very limited (Wilber, 2007: 87). The transrational approach then tries to 'lift' modern truths, in a Hegelian sense,[22] and integrate them with spiritual approaches, which not only opens up possibilities for postmodern interpretations of a multitude of peaces and societies but also to something beyond (Dietrich, 2006b: 37)

---

[21] To be analyzed in chapter four.

[22] The German verb used by Hegel is *aufheben* meaning "to lift", "to preserve". The Hegelian *aufheben* is generally contextualized in the belief that opposites coincide or are reconciled (Inwood, 1992).

1.4.1 Apollo and Dionysius

By taking up Nietzsche's argumentation on Greek tragedy,[23] illustrated in *The Birth of Tragedy from the Spirit of Music*, first published in 1872 (Nietzsche, 2007), Dietrich elaborates on the separation of the Greek Gods of form —Apollo— and Energy —Dionysius— as the starting point for the change from energetic *harmonious* experiences of peace to the moral/modern/postmodern frame of peace conceptualization (Dietrich, 2006b: 43).

Ancient Greeks did not consider the two Gods as opposites or rivals, but with the transformation of society a conceptual change started to take place. With Christianity, for instance, Apollo —the God of form— will later on evolve into the moral and rational concept of the *one truth/rightness/normality* and the God of energy and ecstasy —Dionysius— will evolve into Satan as the personification of the *error/wrongness/abnormality.* Dietrich argues that energy is left behind, *suppressed*, while the empire of form takes over in the Mediterranean world.

With the occurrence of Christianity, the ethos of Apollo was identified with the way of Christ, and Dionysus was relegated to the dark. Apollo and Dionysus at the beginning are like form and energy, but later they are like Christ and Satan, like good and evil. The split between these two realities has created a psychic schism, which has determined the nature of Western civilization. It is crucial that the historic flight from Dionysus in the classic tragedy went hand in hand, as stated before, with the creation and development of the Polis and later the empires in the Mediterranean and their understanding of peace (Dietrich, 2006b: 37).

Apollo, compelled by *Phobos* (fear), drives his excluding and aggressive attitude against everything that smacks of heteronomy (Wilber, 1995: 524). This systematic suppression of Dionysian energy comes to modernity via the modern nation-state and institutionalized religions as a globalized imposition

---

[23] Greek tragedy is a form of art in which performances involve music in the form of choral songs and theater. It was based on the mixture of human suffering and pleasure experienced by the heroic main character and the spectators who were part of the performance and openly expressed their feelings. The play as a whole was composed in various verse meters performed by one, maximum three actors who also sang solos, and a singing and dancing chorus, all used costumes and masks. The largest festival for Greek tragedy was called Great Dionysia in honor of Dionysus, the God of wine and fertility. The presentations took the form of an annual contest among three playwrights chosen by the city, who presented their works on three successive days in Athens. Its origins date back about 2500 years ago (Wiles 1997; Banham 1998).

of conviviality. It opens space for the constant suppression of the "energetic nature and desires within itself and so is reduced to the mere formal, from where it is difficult to imagine energetic realities. Nietzsche calls this habit *the white man's disease*" (Dietrich, 2006b: 37).

Based on the above mentioned philosophical concept of dichotomy, Dietrich brings up to the discussion the protagonist role of suppressed Dionysius in Sigmund Freud's Psychoanalysis, explaining how from there the dichotomy started to be reintegrated by Assagioli's *psycho-synthesis*[24] (1927) and Jung's investigation on the collective unconscious and its functional elements, later on called *archetypes* (Jung, 1969). Citing Jung, Dietrich explains that the psychic condition of an individual depends on manifold interactions with the environment, and that personal experiences would serve to develop the "archetypical potential" of the self because it is a collective legacy of humanity (Dietrich, 2006b: 38).

1.4.2 Quantum Physics and Transpersonal Psychology

Dietrich explains that Jung's archetypes caused great impact in European modern scientists and stimulated curiosity on new understandings of matter and energy. Later, "through the stipulation of Quantum Physics that every single particle carries the information of the whole universe, it also became evident that every human being due to its energetic nature and disposition is a carrier of the complete information of humankind" as Jung suggested. According to this approach, any of this information can be triggered and recalled through experience (Dietrich, 2006b: 39).

It was at this point that psychologists and scientist started to consider more and more seriously that the human psyche and behavior, as well as all material objects, were not exactly *independent*, *individuals*, or *clear units* unlinked from the others as it is understood in the context of Newtonian physics and psychoanalysis, but that they are rather interconnected and share information. Hence, as in the classical myth of Indra,[25] everything that exists is interrelated.

---

[24] As explained by Dietrich (2006a) in "A call for Transrational Peaces", Assagioli is a leading psycho-therapist of the first generation who took Nietzsche's concept of the form-energy Gods and by integrating oriental wisdom into enlightened European tradition demonstrated human potential to constantly integrate complexity and awareness into the state of mind; this was called *psycho-synthesis*.

[25] Indra's Net is a Buddhist metaphor to describe interconnectedness of all beings and phenomena. According to it, when God Indra created the world, it made it as a web and at every

In psychology, this approach was called *Transpersonal* by Abraham Maslow (1971) in the late sixties, having emerged from Humanistic[26] psychology. Dietrich explains that it was mainly developed in the Esalen Institute in California, attracting people like Frederick Perls, Carl Rogers, Stanislav Grof, and Ruth Cohn and scientists of various disciplines like Charles Tart, Roger Walsh, Francis Vaughan, Daisetz Suzuki and peace activists like Erich Fromm, Ivan Illich, Marshall B. Rosenberg, Ervin Laszlo, and Ken Wilber. Paul Goodman, with *Growing up Absurd* (1962), was the early link between these psychologists and the popular peace movement (Dietrich, 2006b: 39-40).

1.4.3 Twisting the Peaces

The twentieth century's scientific notion of connectedness is very similar to the energetic experience of peace by pre-modern so called 'magic' societies as a feeling of *connectedness* with cosmos, nature, and society. Nonetheless, as it comes after humans had been touched by the influence of modernity and postmodernity, it does not refer exactly to that ancient experience of spirituality, but to its *twisting* or integration to the achievements of reason in what Dietrich has called *Transrational Peaces* (Dietrich, 2006a).

Based on Joan Stambaugh's introductory arguments in Heidegger's book *The End of Philosophy and the Task of Thinking* (Heidegger, 1973: 84), Koppensteiner explains how the use of the word *twisting* implies the integration of worldviews using the teachings of each, rather than notions of overcoming or going back romantically to the past; neither is it used in the sense of something that is "defeated", "left behind" or that is "gotten rid of," rather, it has the connotation of incorporating (Koppensteiner, 2009: 19).

---

bond of union in the web there is a pearl. Everything that exists, or has ever existed is a pearl in Indra's net. Not only is every pearl tied to every other by virtue of the web on which they hang, but on the surface of every pearl is reflected every other jewel on the net. Everything that exists in Indra's web implies all else that exists (Brook, 2007).

26 Humanist Psychology criticizes Depth Psychology and Behaviorism for their mechanistic model of cause-effect and anthropological pessimism. Depth Psychology sees the human being as influenced by always problematic impulses and dark desires that arise from the unconscious, this has led to a psychology that only concerns itself with pathology and sickness and is always distrustful and suspicious of parts of the human being. See for instance Bugental and others (2001).

The transrational perspective understands peace as *contextual* and *relational*, as common heritage of and for *all* human beings. All persons have human needs for expressing the complete potential of their feelings, thoughts, words, actions and reactions, because the more these are suppressed in the name of rationality and individuality, the higher is the risk that they return in an uncontrolled, violent and destructive manner (Dietrich 2006a: 17; Koppensteiner, 2009: 203-206).

Conclusion

The philosophy of the *many peaces* has its initial foundations in postmodern thinking. Postmodernism is a theoretical worldview born as an *academic discipline* in Europe in the second half of the nineteenth century. Its roots are placed in disappointment from modernism and refers to the rejection of homogenizing narratives about 'a' universal truth and valid for of *being*. Consequently, it critiques the exclusion of alternative perspectives, of dissenting voices, of coexistent although perhaps contradictory truths.

Some social dynamics in Latin American countries, including Colombia, are also influenced by disillusionment from modern absolute truths. The postmodern stream of thinking served discourses of emancipation of groups that have found themselves in situation of repression and exclusion in different times and places, such as indigenous peoples, women, and the working class, amongst others. Postmodernism gave foundation to discourses against homogenization of identities and influenced creative alternative forms of understanding reality, as such, it was expressed in arts and literature influencing for instance Julio Cortázar's *surrealism* (Cortázar, 1963) and Garcia Marquez's *magical realism* (García Márquez, 1967).

From a postmodern perspective, Dietrich (2006a) criticizes the radicalization of rational explanations of peace that follow the model of *one/absolute* truth and therefore justify the use of violence against diverging groups as means to achieve the one peace based on security. He explains how the modern interpretation of peace is, in fact, only one of the many interpretations in history and culture. Peace based on security takes place in the context of modernity and has a contractual setting, peace in this context is an ideal future *status*. Dietrich categorizes this interpretation as 'modern peace' and enlists it along with other interpretations: the energetic, moral, postmodern and transrational peaces (Dietrich, 2008).

In contrast to the rational model, energetic perspectives of peace are mainly sustained on the spiritual human component. The spiritual component perceives dualities as forming a harmonious whole. It allows the unification of opposites via human emotional capabilities such as empathy and compassion, which can be neither fully explained by rational means, nor enforced via normative conceptualizations. From the energetic perspective, peace is more an attitude than a status.

After presenting a postmodern critic to the conceptualization of the 'one-world' peace and the need to open up for plurality in the concept, Dietrich suggests surrendering to the insufficiency of mere rational means to approach the understanding of peace and conflict matters and proposes a re-integration of the spiritual component present in the energetic interpretation alongside the rational. This reinterpretation of peace is known as the transrational approach to peace which I will use as framework for the upcoming legal analysis.

2. Role of Peace in Legal Theory and Practice

Law and science, two monolithic institutions which generally compete for, but sometimes coincide in presenting, an authoritative analysis of the world.
(Reece, 1998: ix)

Introduction

In the previous chapter, I mentioned that International Peace Research was born in 1919 out of the painful violence experienced during the First World War. On that occasion, academic institutions were established with the aim to find out how to 'fix' violence in the globe, however what followed after World War II was the realization that the century brought escalation of violence instead of a system of one universal peace.

I have also presented some ideas of contemporary peace researchers regarding the conceptualization of 'one universal peace' as a discriminatory practice of modernity and the suggestion to approach peace from a more inclusive-integrative perspective called by Dietrich (2006b, 2009) *Transrational Peaces.* Now I will move toward the analysis of the law from a peace studies perspective, to explore if and how the approach to peace used in the law can be located within this frame.

In regard to my research question —*In the case of conscientious objection to military service in Colombia, how does the interpretation of the right to freedom of conscience vary according to Dietrich's families of interpretation of peace*— in this chapter I will analyze whether diverse cultural conceptions of peace can actually influence and foster changes to the law. Bearing this objective in mind, I will first approach the question 'What is law?' by contrasting different definitions, bringing concepts about the functions of law in society, then examining what is the role of peace within the legal theory and practice and, lastly, questioning what the legal type of peace is and how it is seen from the perspective of Transrational Peaces.

This analysis will be of use for the forthcoming study of the constitutional case of objections to military service, where I will study how different perspectives on peace used by different interpreters of the law can shape diverse interpretations of the right to object military service for reasons of conscience in Colombia.

2.1 What is Law?

Behind the creation and use of law in societies there is an abstract intention of modeling human relations. Legal philosophers from several legal schools such as *Legal Realism, Critical Legal Studies* (CLS) and some branches of *Iuspositivism* and *Iusnaturalism* have been interested in looking at what are the intentions or purposes behind the use of legal systems. The link between law and culture has been explored in that search.

Notably, it is important to understand the scope and limits of the law because legal rules have somehow become omnipresent in the daily life of modern societies (Atienza, 2000). There is almost no social relation, which is not legally regulated or can become legally regulated. According to Atienza, the *legal* aspect is only one of the many aspects of social life, yet it has become essential (Atienza, 2000: 5).

To verify his statement the author (Atienza 2000) picks up a random newspaper whose headlines are: the hijacking of an airplane; permission for therapeutic use of hashish from a judge in Barcelona and release of a detainee; and, reduction of electricity charge for next year and failure in dialogue between ETA and the Spanish government, all the events somehow relevant to the law. They all constitute either a crime, are regulated by administrative or international norms, or can have potential for compensation claims.

To focus on more personal experiences, Atienza also comments that the daily life of many people is also surrounded by legally regulated situations such us transport contracts every time they take a bus, administrative regulated acts when they register as students in a public university, pay taxes, or get a traffic fine (Atienza, 2000: 6-8). Some of the intentions behind the law focus on bringing structure and order to human social relations. It is essential to minimize the risk of damages like in the case of traffic lights, traffic speed limits, control of food prices, recycling, insurances, use of water, gas and electricity, distribution of welfare, access to public health and many more. All these situations function within organized normative systems. Not surprisingly peace and war are legally regulated as well.

Additionally, the unfolding of people's full potentials and identities is subject of legal regulations as well. This is the case of sexual preferences, family, the contract of marriage, participation in national or international wars, and expression of religious beliefs just to pick some. All these topics are important to people´s everyday life, relevant to peace and violence and are regulated by law. But, why so? What is the law and what are the limits of legal regulation?

My initial intention with this chapter was to start with a good definition of law and then take the peace studies analysis from there. But I soon found myself in trouble. Finding a definition of law that is comprehensive enough to describe the complex web of human *legal* relations is difficult. Paraphrasing Einstein, Alchourrón and Bulygin explain that "as far as concepts refer to reality, they are not certain, and as far as they are certain, they do not refer to reality" (Alchourrón & Bulygin, 2006: 63) and this seems to be the case for concepts on law. Having difficulties in concisely explaining what law is about I realized that this frustration could probably be a first element to defining the legal phenomenon as a normative structure that is meant to be essentially relational, as Duncan Kennedy states when referring to legal education in universities:

> [T]he class context and the materials present every legal issue as distinct from every other —as a tub on its own bottom, so to speak— with no hope or even any reason to hope that from law study one might derive an integrating vision of what law is, how it works, or how it might change (other than in an incremental, case-by- case, reformist way). (Kennedy, 1990: 59)

Etymologically, the English word *law* derives from the old English *lagu* of Scandinavian origin, which was the plural of lag 'laying, good order' and the Proto-Indo-European root legh (to lay) that means "something laid down or fixed" (Skeat, 1993). Law has always been difficult to define by jurists, because, to start with, it has the semantic characteristic of *ambiguity* (Suárez 2002). "The term *right* like the term *law* is polysemic and ambiguous, and the two terms often overlap" (Engle, 2010: 85), the ambiguity of the word implies that it can be used to refer to different concepts or meanings depending on the context.

Besides, according to Atienza (1985: 10), law can have multiple meanings according to the perspective from which it is looked at; this is why different definitions seem to be referring to different concepts or at least to different aspects of law. While some definitions focus on describing the structure of legal systems, others focus more on the functions or social values pursued by law. Facing this strain, I will approach a working definition by exploring various perspectives on law.

2.1.1 Structural, Functional and Value-System Perspectives on Law

Following Atienza, Suárez (2002) explains how, for instance, the definitions of law by three classic authors: Thomas Aquinas, Karl Marx and Hans Kelsen vary a lot from each other, which shows the influence of their ideological and historical backgrounds. Thus, while Aquinas defines law as the *ordina-*

tion of reason aimed at the common good, Marx sees it as an *instrument for domination of one class over another* and Kelsen simply as a *set of coercive rules*. From Atienza's examples, it is possible to see at least three different perspectives from which to define law: (1) its structure, (2) its function or role in society and (3) the value system it pursues (Suárez, 2002: 11-13).

Structural Perspective

From a structural perspective, law is defined according to what it is objectively composed of — its elements. Consequently, it is understood as a *set of rules of conduct.* According to Suárez (2002: 13), Kelsen's normativist understanding would be the clearest example of a structural definition of law.[27] Considering that there are other sets of regulation of human conduct besides the legal i.e. *religious, moral, customary* and *ethical* rules, legal philosophers such as Del Vecchio (1946), Máynez (1974) and Bobbio (1998) have tried to distinguish legal rules from other rules of conduct by pointing out their distinctive characteristics, namely:

(1) Legal rules refer to *external-social conduct,* not to thoughts or mere private actions which do not affect other people in a clear cause-effect manner; (2) they are *coactive*, meaning enforceable or compulsory under the threat of sanction by a public authority and, (3) they are *bilateral* in the sense that connect two persons or groups in a co-relational manner. In this vein, one person's *right* implies a *duty* for other and vice-versa. Unifying the mentioned characteristics, from the structural perspective law is defined as a *set of bilateral and coactive rules of human social conduct.*

Functional Perspective

From a functional perspective, law is explained in reference to the role legal rules have in societies, which has been and still is polemic amongst political and social scientists. It is possible to identify several types of perceptions

[27] Hans Kelsen (1881-1973) was an Austrian jurist of high relevance for legal studies especially in continental Europe and Latin America, who adopted the method of analyzing law from a scientific approach, observing rules as 'objective' elements of legal systems that exist and are valid with independence of social ideas of justice. The validity of rules according to Kelsen's perspective depends only on the rules of validity existent within concrete legal systems, then judges and other jurists' role is to apply norms objectively by using the rules of logic.

about what is that which law *brings to* or *takes from* society. There are at least two main streams: one considers law as a positive social element for organization and the other one considers law as a negative tool of mere domination. Suárez (2002: 23) thinks that these types are related to different interpretations of society itself, which he categorizes as *functionalist* and *conflictivist.*

On the one hand, authors such as Durkheim, Weber, Parsons and Luhmann, are functionalists, they offer a vision of society as a system composed of several elements that are in equilibrium and happened to coordinate themselves to keep in balance. This balance is understood as social control. Within this frame, law is understood as an essential mechanism to achieve and keep that equilibrium, and to bring positive values needed by societies such as security, conflict resolution, and the guarantee of equality and freedom (Suárez, 2002: 23-24).

Elaborating on the work of Máynez (1974), Suárez explains how law would then be a mechanism used by society to reduce the occurrence of conducts previously considered as equilibrium breakers or *illegal*, and to facilitate conducts which would be those seen by a community as desired according to its value system, or *legal* (Suárez, 2002: 23). In this vein, Máynez (1974) argues that *law* is a system of social control, or mechanism to achieve and maintain social order by virtue of preventing conflicts, or where appropriate, of resolving them.

On the other hand, *conflictivists* like Marx see society not as a system in balance that coordinates itself, but rather as a system characterized by chaos, inequality, instability and class struggle. In this sense law's function within this system is to *maintain the struggle via domination of one class above another* and justifying capitalist exploitation through the guise of a supposed equality and freedom; according to this viewpoint, law has *ideological and dominant functions in society* (Suárez, 2002: 25). To conclude, a definition of law according to its function in society varies fundamentally depending on the author and political stream of thought.

Value-System Perspective

Lastly, from a value-system perspective, law is defined "according to the social values it pursues or in which it is to find its foundations" (Suárez, 2002: 25). There is no general agreement regarding legal values, neither concerning what they represent in the present, nor about what they should be like. The field of legal axiology concentrates the vast debate in this regard.

"The issue of values is one of the great questions that philosophy raises in relation to law" (Suárez 2008: 26).

A classic definition where a value is a central element is Aquinas' understanding of law as the *ordination of reason aimed at the common good* (Aquinas quoted in Suárez, 2008: 26). More recent authors also understand law by referring directly to the value of justice, for instance as a *tool, or set of them, and a way to use them in the effort to move closer to justice* (Nieto & Fernández, 1998: 20). Notably, the primary value to which legal literature refers to is *justice,* and from it other values of equal importance derive, such as common good, equality, and social peace. For the United Nations justice is:

> [A]n ideal of accountability and fairness in the protection and vindication of rights and the prevention and punishment of wrongs. Justice implies regard for the rights of the accused, for the interests of victims and for the well-being of society at large. It is a concept rooted in all national cultures and traditions and, while its administration usually implies formal judicial mechanisms, traditional dispute resolution mechanisms are equally relevant. The international community has worked to articulate collectively the substantive and procedural requirements for the administration of justice for more than half a century. (UN Security Council, 2004)

Even though the idea of justice has been the key element for the growth of legal institutions, it is an abstract value whose content is relational, changes from case to case. In the words of Nieto and Fernandez a broad definition of justice is "unattainable and elusive" (Nieto & Fernández, 1998: 59) because it's meaning is contextual and always changing.

Sometimes we hear the variation "peace and justice," which refers to something abstract in the future or the past but never in the present (Dietrich 2009). When looking at past situations when communities felt threatened in their security, performed injustice or found themselves trapped by erratic actions, then the establishment of norms offers future salvation from such adverse situations and promises *peace* if —and only if— people follow the institutions and obey the norms. Thus, "peace and justice" are subject to the obedience of general norms (Dietrich 2009).

To conclude, some definitions of law focus on values that are to be achieved by its use, *justice* is the primary value referred to in legal literature, and from it other important values derive, frequently common good, equality, and social peace. Now, why create laws at all? What intentions or ideas lead communities to create legally binding norms at specific times? Two main streams of interpretation in legal philosophy have approached this issue: Iusnaturalism and Positivism.

2.1.2 Classic Ideas on Law: Iusnaturalism and Iuspositivism

Iusnaturalism

Iusnaturalism is a school of legal philosophy characterized for particular understandings of the *source* of legal rules. For Iusnaturalists, legal norms obey a human shared (universal) knowledge on justice and harmony of relations. Thus, legal norms that contradict that shared knowledge are unjust and therefore illegitimate.

There are historical variations of Iusnaturalism offering spiritual, religious and rational perspectives. Classic Iusnaturalists such as Tomas Aquinas claimed that the universal laws of justice are revealed to humans by God. From a different angle, Rational Iusnaturalists —such as Groccio, Hobbes, Rousseau, Ruffendorf and Kant— claim those shared laws of justice to be accessible by reason through the knowledge of human nature (Suárez, 2002).

Following Nino (1980a), the different streams of Iusnaturalism have two things in common: the first is the belief in universal unwritten rules of justice or harmonious relations common to all humans and the second is the establishment of a condition for law to exist as such. This means that law must be fair in order to exist. For Iusnaturalists, an unfair rule (one which does not correspond to universal unwritten rules of justice) simply does not receive the status of 'legal'; it is invalid and as such, has no binding effects for people.

The struggle for relating law to *justice/injustice* is reflected already in the lines of Sophocles' Antigone dating 442 BC (Sophocles, 2008), where Antigone, being confronted by the contradiction of the *law of humans* and the *law that gods write in human spirit*, defies Creon's decree that her brother should remain unburied. Antigone proclaims the law of the gods instead of the one of humans in defense of "her own conscience and human dignity" (Suárez, 2002: 28).

Iuspositivism

Iuspositivism for its part does not condition the existence of legal norms to its correspondence to the common idea of harmony or justice. According to Nino (1980a: 33), Bobbio explains this idea by saying that *law is fair just for the fact of being law*. Furthermore, for Iuspositivists there is no such a thing as a common principle of justice or superior harmonious unwritten laws influencing written norms.

Iuspositivism was mostly developed in continental Europe by the end of the nineteenth century and beginning of the twentieth with Hans Kelsen as its most recognized author with his text *Pure Theory of Law* (Kelsen, 1978). Norms are understood as neutral and objective. Ideas of inspirational values and the analysis of what law should be like and how it ought to be transformed are not relevant in determining the validity of norms. From this perspective, the analysis of law is approached in a strict *scientific* manner.

The law is no more than the written norms and they are separate from principles and morals. This is why Iuspositivists have been related to ethical skepticism (Suárez, 2002: 36). The French Iuspositivist Jean-Joseph Bugnet said, "*I do not explain law, I explain the code*" (Bugnet quoted in Huertas 2006: 1) in reference to the set of rules contained in Civil Code of 1804. According to Huertas (2006), Bugnet's is a perfect explanation for the meaning of extreme positivism.

However, not all legal positivism is to be related to ethical skepticism. Many positivists such as Bentham (1823), Ross (2004), Hart (1961, 1983) and Austin (2009) analyzed the interrelation between laws and social values while still conditioning law's validity strictly to the fulfillment of legal requirements. What all these authors share is:

> The conception that the law is a factual or social phenomenon which can be identified and described by an external observer without adopting a position about its moral justification or the moral duty to observe it. They emphasize that one can and should distinguish the law that 'is' from the law that 'ought to be'. (Nino, 1980b: 520)

Dworkin (1977, 1996) disagrees with the idea of the *objective lawyer* and goes deeply into the essential role of values in the creation and interpretation of rights in the United States' legal system. Dworkin claims the insufficiency of the law to solve conflictive situations and refers to the key function of the jurist's political values when filling loopholes or balancing rights and duties. Dworkin claims himself to be a *natural* lawyer or Iusnaturalist, even though his texts and views are considered by many to correspond with Iuspositivism.

In other words, while Iusnaturalism considers that written rules come from a universal understanding of harmony or justice shared by all humnas, Iuspositivism turns the argument upside down considering that justice comes from written legal rules. As any other dualism these two possible interpretations of legal axiology have led to many academic and politic argumentations, contradictions, and developments.

Considering the pluralistic approach in which I am framing this research work, I would like to avoid emphasizing the logical contradiction between Iusnaturalism and Iuspositivism, merely apparent if following Gödel's incompleteness models mentioned earlier. Hence, I will rather point out the existence of various approaches to the meaning of legal rules according to vernacular value systems.

2.1.3 Tamanaha's Clusters of Meaning

Going beyond the black and white assessment of law's function in society as being either positive (it brings order) or negative (it brings domination), Tamanaha (2004: 137-141) holds the analysis referring to a rainbow of influences and meanings of legal practices with variations amongst different cultures. He calls these *clusters of meaning* for the rule of law,[28] and uses them to approach the query *is law a universal human good?* In accordance to Tamanaha some possible meanings of law are: Controlling the ones in power, predictability, and "Rule of Law, Not Man."

"Controlling the ones in power"

The first cluster of meaning refers to law signifying that *the government is limited to exercising its power* (including a limitation for law making). As there is a need for controlling the ones in power in almost all societies, the great contribution of the rule of law to human existence in this sense is that it provides one answer to that need. Having mentioned that, Tamanaha elaborates on the issue of plurality by pointing out that limiting governments' power may be a universal human need but the limits themselves are not universal at all. "Protection of human needs against excess of power from others was a concern in ancient Athens, a concern throughout the medieval period and continues to be a concern everyday today" (Tamanaha, 2004: 139). However, the precise limits established to protect human needs against excess of power from others can vary a lot amongst cultures, thus trying to universalize them brings daunting complications (Tamanaha, 2004).

---

[28] The English concept Rule of Law equals to the Spanish *Estado de Derecho*, used in the Colombian political Constitution in its form of *Estado Social de Derecho*; which means the equal submission to law of all persons and public/private institutions including the State itself. The addition of the social component to the rule of law implies the idea of not aiming at mere order when using law (respect for the law) but to human dignity in every concrete case (respect for people).

Predictability

Tamanaha's second cluster of meaning is framed by *Formal Legality,* meaning that the law provides security in the sense of *predictability.* Tamanaha refers to predictability as a supremely valuable good, "but not necessarily a universal human good" (Tamanaha, 2004: 139) since some cultures may consider it less important than others. Predictability here refers to situations where the government threatens people with the use of force against them, especially in the imposition of criminal sanctions. Tamanaha also mentions the importance of predictability of transactions, commercial and market among strangers or members of different communities.

Nonetheless, formal legality may not need to be applied if other "functionally equivalent social mechanisms are efficacious, as when relationships and prevailing cultural understandings generate security and predictability" (Tamanaha, 2004: 139), especially in the case of families, non-liberal cultures or hybrid cultures. When liberal and non-liberal orientations circulate, the proper application of formal legality can be determined only in the context at hand, by the people involved, otherwise it will inflict harm being disruptive of relationships and social bonds.

"Rule of Law, not Persons"

The third cluster of meaning is *the rule of law, not persons* aiming at the avoidance of tyranny, dictatorship and domination. Tamanaha explains that this element follows whenever the first or second clusters of meaning are adopted. In other words, when a society embraces the idea that the ones in power are limited by some rules, it satisfies the qualities of predictability and control over governments (Tamanaha, 2004). According to the United Nations (UN), the rule of law refers to:

> [A] principle of governance in which all persons, institutions and entities, public and private, including the state itself, are accountable to laws that are publicly promulgated, equally enforced and independently adjudicated. (UN Security Council, 2004)

This element connects law to democracy and is most valuable in Human Rights Law, however, it is important to be aware of its limits. Accepting the rule of law with radical devotion, may imply an idealistic understanding of state-officers and judges acting with absolute objectivity and only speaking the voice of law. This position has been strongly criticized for being inconvenient and unrealizable under the argument that state-officers and judges are human beings, and will be always subjective. Besides, written rules are abstract and always need adaptation to the concrete case, for which it is fundamental to resort to human creativity.[29]

2.1.4 Which are the actual laws to follow?

The former definitins of law describe the structure of binding norms, perspectives on their functions in society and some of the social values they aim to model. Now, modern societies are characterized by extensive legal regulations of many kinds in a way that it is not easy to know which norms apply for what situation and when. In complex societies so full of regulations, which are the actual norms to be applied? How to know which are the established limits of human actions? In *El derecho y el revés,* Nieto & Fernández (1998) illustrate the challenges they encounter as professors of law when reflecting upon legal theory in contrast to legal practice. One of the realizations they recount is how the conception of what the law is and how it is used can actually vary significantly.

What defines the content of norms? Schools of thought in legal studies talk about at least four possibilities: law is what written rules say, what judges say, what legal principles say, and lastly, laws are created and re-created by constant process of argumentation, acts of language that happen between concrete people in concrete situations. These possibilities are not necessarily mutually exclusive but may interplay in court cases. Later in chapter four, I will use these perspectives to argue that processes of argumentation about the meanings of peace and security in Colombia inform not only the creation of new laws but also new interpretations and ways of using already existing norms.

Law is what rules say

Law is the code and the code is law, the interpreter does not influence the norm. Legal studies follow the rules of applied sciences in the sense of observation and objectivity. The legal school developing this position is *legal positivism* or *Iuspositivism* also known as *legal formalism* as explained earlier. Following a belief in objectivity, Positivists commonly use expressions

---

[29] For a critique see Jueces de Mármol (marble judges) (Nanclares 2001); Legal schools such as Legal Realism and Critical Legal Studies (CLS) approach legal analysis as always interconnected to economics, politics and sociology and support the idea of complete objectivity as an impossibility in legal contexts.

such as 'legal science' and 'legal engineering'. Proponents of legal formalism say that law is what is commanded by a lawgiver, that judges are not lawgivers, and that what judges do, while it might belong to the field of law, is not "law" but legal practice.

Law is what judges say

Some legal scholars have developed the idea that the background, value system, and political preferences of legal practicioners make them interpret rules in different manners; consequently, cases may be decided differently even if they refer to the application of the same rule. According to this viewpoint, law ends up being judges' subjective interpretations of what rules say. *Legal realism* is the legal school elaborating this perspective: it was developed in the first half of the twentieth century in the United States (known as *American legal realism*) and Scandinavia (*Scandinavian legal realism*). Legal Realism worked vigorously to portray the institution of law without denying or distorting a picture of sharp moral, political, and social conflict. The most important legacy of Legal Realism is its challenge to the classical legal claim that legal reasoning was separate and autonomous from moral and political discourse (Fisher, Horwitz, & Reed, 1993).

Many of the legal realists believe that the law in the books does not determine the results of legal disputes. Jerome Frank (1973) famously quoted that a judicial decision might be determined by *what the judge had for breakfast*. Part of the realist school is the importance of interdisciplinary approaches to law. Legal realists use sociological and anthropological approaches to the legal study and belief in legal instrumentalism. It is the view that the law should be used as a tool (one of many) to balance competing societal interests. The essential view of this school is that law is made by humans and is therefore subject to human changes and imperfections. The postulates of legal realism will be of relevance for the upcoming analysis of the role of perspectives on peace in the argumentation of the right to object to military service in Colombia.

Law is what legal principles say

Considering the permanent creation of legal rules at all levels it becomes more difficult for jurists to find the proper rule to apply in concrete cases; in this context *legal principles* define how to use law (Nieto & Fernández, 1998: 13). Principles are intended to be used in case of loopholes or interpret legal rules whose application is questionable. Atienza argues that principles "lend meaning to the normative institutions or sectors" (Atienza & Ruiz, 1991: 117).

Ávila (2007) explains that legal *principles* guide or point to the grounds that a jurist can use in order to find the rule that applies to the concrete case. Following Larenz, Ávila shows how from a hypothetical-conditional viewpoint principles can be distinguished from rules as they are "norms of great relevance for the legal order inasmuch as they set forth normative foundations for the interpretation and application of the law, therefrom evolving whether directly or indirectly behavior norms" (Ávila, 2007: 11-12).

Principles have a tensioning position between norms and values and as such, according to authors of the contemporary Anglo-American legal philosophy (Critical Legal Studies and Legal Realism) such as Dworkin (1977, 1996). *Principles* show the permanent connection between social values or issues of public policy and rules, which positivists see as 'objective' elements. The authors in the current of Anglo-American legal philosophy mentioned here put forward once again the discussion about *Iusnaturalism and Iuspositivism* present at the beginning of the twentieth century, intending to show that law is never objective, never closed off from social ideals of justice/injustice and peace/violence as strong streams of *Iuspositivism* had interpreted it. On the contrary, they claim that those values do influence the manner in which jurists actually interpret and use law in every concrete case.

In the same vein, Atienza and Ruiz (1991) explain how the role of principles in legal argumentation is less binding but at the same time can be more powerful than rules in the sense that they have a broader justificatory scope. Principles do not establish something mandatory to do, but reasons to interpret and use legal systems in certain ways.

Following this interpretation and considering that the Colombian Constitution establishes plurality, respect of human dignity, peaceful coexistence and protection of the ethnic and cultural diversity as fundamental *principles* of the legal system (*Constitution of Colombia*, 1991: Title I), my argument is that jurists' own perspective on peace and their personal ideas about the role of plurality in relation to peace, directly influence the way in which they build legal argumentation of rights. In other words, different perspectives on peace influence different argumentation of rights. The *philosophy of the many peaces* can be considered a principle to be applied in legal argumentation in Colombia.

Law is argumentation: practical-justificatory reasoning

The idea of law as argumentation is developed by Atienza in *El Derecho como Argumentación* (Atienza, 1999, 2006). The author explores the argumentative dimension of law and nails the point home that argumentation is not the only dimension of law, even though it is a comprehensive one. The starting point is to look at law as a technique for the solution of certain practical problems. For Atienza, understanding law as argumentation means to look at it from the perspective of "someone who is engaged with the task of improving an imperfect and always unfinished work, but not for that reason meaningless" (Atienza, 1999: 38).

Law as argumentation comes from the assumption that the regulative ideal of the rule of law is the subjection of power to reason, not of reason to power. Therefore, the decisions made by public authorities should be based on reasonable arguments (which is only possible if we accept some kind of objectivity in this practice). Law can be seen as a complex net of decisions linked to the solution of certain practical problems. But in the law of democratic societies, what matters are not only the decisions but *the reasons* —or certain types of reasons— offered in favor to make those decisions (Atienza, 1999). Taking Atienza's point into account, the respect of a plurality of peaces can be used as a reason offered in favor of pluralistic interpretation of rights.

Atienza (1999) explains that there is no one and only understanding of what it is to argue or what arguments are. But he talks about three main components of argumentation: the logic, the material and the pragmatic. The first is based on following rules of logic: chains of propositions guiding to valid inferences, which, to Atienza, more than arguments, seem to be schemes of argumentation, very useful in legal practice especially in the task of *judging*, but never *sufficient*. Logical argumentation is linked to the idea of *predictability,* a transversal concept within the theory of law, as explained by Tamanaha (2004).

The *material* component of argumentation is based on notions of *justice* or *truth*. Atienza explains the existence of *reasons for action*; the many possible reasons that we have for acting how we do and the ways of working out conflicts amongst those reasons to finally decide how to act. Material argumentation goes down to the *content* of the reasons we use for action. They imply some kind of moral and political philosophy therefore they are not only formal (Atienza, 1999: 44). Considering the abstract content of values, this point can be linked to the idea that "legal thought can generate equally plausible rights justifications for almost any result" (Kennedy, 1990: 62).

The third or *pragmatic* component, also called dialectic by Atienza (1999), sees argumentation as a type of action or *linguistic interaction*, as a complex act of language that happens between concrete people in concrete situations. Thus, it is a *process* depending on some rules of linguistic behavior of the persons involved and insofar the pragmatic aspect of language cannot be ignored. From this view, the argumentation cannot be conceived with independence of the persons who argue.

The process of argumentation develops as intervenors start making concessions. Inferring consists in moving from one statement to the other by acceptance and consensus. Premises would be those whose acceptance is presupposed by all intervenors or for being achieved at every step in the process and the conclusion is whatever is aimed to be accepted by the other (Atienza, 1999: 44). The three components of argumentation are not incompatible but rather complementary, thus an adequate theory on legal argumentation should consider them all (Atienza, 1999).

2.1.5 Perspective of the ONIC

To conclude this section on the meaning of law, I would like to include the perspective of the National Indigenous Organization of Colombia (ONIC), who provides an account on the meaning of normative systems from an energetic-oriented perspective. In contrast to modern/postmodern accounts on law that refer to law mainly as a creation of human reason, the indigenous concept of normative systems integrates the spiritual component that characterizes energetic perspectives on peace (Dietrich, 2008). This approach will be relevant in chapter four, where I will analyze how different perspectives on peace shape variations in the argumentation of rights. According to the National Indigenous Organization of Colombia:

> *Los sistemas jurídicos propios [indígenas] constituyen sistemas de derecho [...] integrados por las normas, instituciones, usos y costumbres y procedimientos, métodos de control y regulación social propios de la tradición cultural de los pueblos indígenas, implícitos en su historia cultural, concepción espiritual, mitología y cosmovisión particulares, en sus sistemas de parentesco, formas de propiedad, uso, aprovechamiento y conservación de sus territorios y recursos naturales.*
>
> *Se caracterizan por concepciones particulares de derecho, justicia, autoridad y poder, participación y representación, mediadas por instituciones culturales propias y determinadas por los principios de armonía social, espiritual con la naturaleza y en equilibrio de fuerzas.*
>
> *Los conceptos indígenas sobre derecho están basados en una profunda ética de relación gente-naturaleza y en su conocimiento de las fuerzas espirituales o*

> *sagradas y en relación con autoridades-equilibrio y armonía. Su principal fuente es la historia cultural propia, contenidas en las palabras de su antiguo o de raíz que conservan en la memoria de los sabios culturales.*[30] (ONIC in Decision T-113/09: 14)

Having reviewed the meaning of law from different perspectives and some of the multiple ideas standing behind the legalization of human actions, in the next subsection I will deepen into the connecting points between peace and law. The following analysis will be the foundation of the idea of pluralistic interpretations of rights for the facilitation of cultures of peace in Colombia, to be developed in chapter four.

2.2 Role of Peace in Legal Theory and Practice

Peace inspires the creation and use of legal institutions in all its dimensions mentioned above (subsection 2.1): the political/legal process of creating legal *norms* (law as norm), how *judges decide* legal conflicts (law as fact), the content jurists give to *legal principles* (law as value), and how people *argue* their legal claims and decisions (law as argumentation). My argument here is that the most relevant topics of peace studies are transversal to legal theory and practice. Thus, jurists' awareness of topics of international Peace Research is of high importance for the transformation of legal systems towards non-violent practices.

Using the above-mentioned notion of law as argumentation within its *formal, material* and *political* dimensions, legal argumentation is, as explained by Atienza (1999) a *process*, it never ends, and it has no particular formula.

---

[30] [Indigenous] own legal systems are systems of law [...] composed by rules, institutions, customs, uses and procedures, methods of social control and regulation according to indigenous peoples' cultural traditions. They are based on a particular cultural history, spiritual notion, mythology and cosmology of the indigenous communities, as well as in their kinship systems, forms of ownership, use, development and conservation of their territories and natural resources. They are characterized by particular conceptions of law, justice, authority and power, participation and representation, mediated by their own cultural institutions and determined by their principles of social harmony, spiritual nature and the balance of forces. Indigenous concepts of law are based on a profound ethical people-nature relationship and their knowledge of the sacred or spiritual forces in relation with the balance of authorities and harmony. Its main source is its own cultural history contained in the words of its ancient root, preserved in the memory of the cultural wisdom (ONIC in Decision T-113/09: 14). Translation by the author.

It is rather a linguistic exchange in permanent transformation, in which jurists use a plurality of elements, namely:

(1) The use of *formal rules of logic* and techniques to deal with legal systems. It is a technical skill that jurists learn, for which they are trained in university as plumbers are trained to deal with pipes.

(2) The *material approach to legal values and principles* used to interpret and give axiological meaning to every other rule of any legal area (for example, criminal, tort, family, contracts, economics and administrative law, to name a few). For this task jurists get some guidance in university with subjects such as legal sociology, legal anthropology, history, legal axiology and ethics, among others. But also the personal background and personality of the jurist are of strong influence[31] in how they interpret and use legal principles, and

(3) The *pragmatic/political* values involved in legal argumentation related to social acceptance. The tension of power and jurists' identification to political parties or other associations of civil society play an important role in what kind of *reasons* judges use to decide cases, lawyers use to defend clients, congressmen and women use to promote the creation of new rules or eliminate existent ones, and members of government use to justify public spending or public management strategies, for instance. In addition, the issue of acceptance and recognition has an impact in what kind of *concessions and agreements* jurists are willing to do in the process of legal argumentation with their counterparts (Atienza 1999: 44-45).

The social image and position a jurist has and aims to have in society is affected by her/his way of using legal argumentation in favor of specific legal values or sets of values. The same applies for a particular interpretation of peace as legal value; it has a political impact and influences a jurist's personal life. There is no training in university on how to deal with the struggle for social acceptance in the context of legal practice, and, once again, no formula whatsoever.

Peace thus, has several roles in the legal theory and practice. It is a *principle* in some national legal systems such as the Colombian and the international system of human rights' protection.[32] Jurists use principles in case of

---

[31] For detailed study of how liberal and conservative sets of values give different material content to laws, see Kennedy (2002).

[32] See the reference to peace in the preamble to the Colombian Constitution (Constitution of Colombia, 1991). Also the first paragraph of the Universal Declaration of Human Rights says: "recognition of the inherent dignity and of the equal and inalienable rights of all members of the human family is the foundation of freedom, justice and peace in the world"

loopholes and when balancing rights and duties. Furthermore, peace is a legal *value*, which means that it inspires general legal doctrine and creation of norms (Barraca Mairal, 2005) and also a concrete *right and duty* within the Colombian legal system, and probably in others.[33] *Peace* is also the main aim of any legal trial, literature on procedural law refers to court cases as ultimately conducted to restore social peace (Devis Echandía, 2004: 195).

Considering the transversal role of peace for legal studies, interestingly peace has been understood by Nieto & Fernández (1998: 58) as the *main value and aim of law,* instead of justice. They maintain that there is a need for removing the topic of justice from the legal practice because *peace* is what law really is about. According to them, law's main role is to try to enable *peaceful* situations in concrete cases of conflict. Consequently they give *peace* a protagonist role within the law:

> *[El] derecho es siempre fruto de un diálogo múltiple que parte y pretende llegar a un consenso más o menos general, pero en cualquier caso suficiente, que no se logra de una vez para siempre y que por el contrario se encuentra permanentemente infieri y demanda por ello un esfuerzo continuo de renovación por parte de todos los operadores jurídicos, que es tanto como decir todos los individuos que componen una sociedad dada. Ese esfuerzo colectivo y permanente de alimentación y reconstrucción del consenso que crea y sostiene las normas es imprescindible, porque allí donde falte, o en la medida en que falte, tendrá que ser suplido por la fuerza, ya que sin normas no es posible la convivencia en paz.*[34] (Nieto & Fernández, 1998: 27)

Legal practices are relative and gravitate around the peace/violence tension. In this regard, Nieto and Fernández (1998) comment that legal philosophies are attempts to give global explanations about law, all of them have both succeeded and failed. All of them have tried to find *the* ultimate solution or

(Universal Declaration of Human Rights, 1948). In both norms peace constitutes a legal principle of use in case of interpretation of any other rule of the Constitution or universal charter.

33 Article 22, Colombian Constitution: "La paz es un deber y una obligación de obligatorio cumplimiento" (Peace is a Right and a duty whose compliance is mandatory) (Constitution of Colombia, 1991: Article 22).

34 "Law is always the result of multifold dialogue; it starts from and aims to reach a consensus more or less general, but in any case sufficient. It is not accomplished once and forever, on the contrary, it is permanently in fieri and demands continuous renewal by all legal operators, which is like saying all the individuals who compose a given society. Collective efforts to bring permanent feeding and reconstruction of the consensus that creates and maintains the standards is essential, because where it is missing or to the degree in which it is missing, it has to be reinstated by force, because without rules there can be no coexistence in peace" (Nieto & Fernández, 1998: 27). Translation by the author.

explanation. The imagination of millions and millions of legal practitioners acting in any society is inexhaustible and the numbers of challenges law can present are infinite. Legal systems and theories can only provide partial solutions, structures and viewpoints which are useful in helping us comprehend a complex changeable reality; permanently, we find ourselves within that reality having to make decisions that allow us to live in *peace* (Nieto & Fernández, 1998: 29-30).

The Colombian Constitutional Court has also referred to the core role of peace for the law in the case of Colombia:

> *La Paz constituye (i) uno de los propósitos fundamentales del Derecho Internacional; (ii) un fin fundamental de Estado colombiano; (iii) un derecho colectivo en cabeza de la Humanidad, dentro de la tercera generación de derechos; (iv) un derecho subjetivo de cada uno de los seres humanos individualmente considerados; y (v), un deber jurídico de cada uno de los ciudadanos colombianos, a quienes les corresponde propender a su logro y mantenimiento.*[35] (Decision C-370/06: 281)

And most importantly for the argument of this book, the Colombian Constitutional Court has sustained that peace cannot be taken as an absolute value that justifies any kind of public policy, on the contrary, it is to be valued contextually, considering the particular needs of people involved in each case:

> *Pero la paz no lo justifica todo. Al valor de la paz no se le puede conferir un alcance absoluto, ya que también es necesario garantizar la materialización del contenido esencial del valor de la justicia y del derecho de las víctimas a la justicia.*[36] (Constitutional Court in Decision C-370/06: 281)

2.3 LEGAL TYPE OF PEACE: THE MODERN

Modern notions of peace are built on the belief that the entire world can be scientifically determined, thus corresponding recipes for action to implement peace can then be derived. Dietrich explains how, as a consequence there is

---

[35] "Peace constitutes (i) one of the fundamental aims of International Law; (ii) a fundamental aim of the Colombian State; (iii) a collective right of all humanity within the third generation of rights; (iv) an individual right; and (v), a legal duty of all Colombian citizens, who are expected to contribute to its achievement and maintenance" (Constitutional Court in Decision C-370/06: 281). Translation by the author.

[36] "But peace cannot justify all kind of political actions. Peace as a value cannot be given an absolute meaning, because it is necessary to guarantee the concrete materialization of the essential content of the value of justice and law for the victims of justice" (Constitutional Court in Decision C-370/06: 281). Translation by the author.

the belief that *we can make peace*; we can make *paradise on earth.* The Hobbesian nation-state is built on the precepts of the absolute power of a strong state which ensures order on the inside and protects its citizens from an outside perceived as hostile and anarchic (Dietrich, 2008).

Modern notions of peace are oriented towards abstract concepts of security, justice, morals and norms. The concept of *Peace* is present in discourses of legal theory and practice concretely in the form of *social peace* in the context of the nation-state. As mentioned earlier in this chapter, legal doctrine asserts that legal rules are distinguished from other kind of rules of human conduct since, among other characteristics, they refer to *social* conduct, which means, to human actions that affect the sphere of other persons rather than mere private behavior that only affects the self:

> *La paz es a la vez un valor, un fin y un bien para el derecho. La paz constituye un valor en el que el derecho hace participar a la convivencia social, por medio de la justicia. La paz que interesa específicamente al derecho es la paz social, la paz de la sociedad humana en cuanto comunidad (y no por ejemplo la paz interior personal o la paz de la conciencia).*[37] (Barraca Mairal, 2005: 133)

I would like to challenge the idea of *one social peace* as a value, asset and end of law, as explained by Barraca Mairal (2005). For instance, the concept of *harm* in which law finds the core base of its protective rights and compensatory rules, is culturally/contextually defined: what for a person or group may be understood as damaging could be of high value for others. One example would be polygamy. For some, like particular Bedouins, polygamy confers prestige as a sign of wealth and prowess, while for some other cultures it is consider a crime against the family institution, as it was in Colombia until 2001 (*Decree-Law 100/80*). Before 2001, polygamy in Colombia was considered a crime with penalty of imprisonment, because it was seen as an offense against legal values such as stability, transparency and loyalty to the family institution (Constitutional Court in Decision C-659/97).

Civil rights and their counterpart prohibitions are linked to what Maslow in his pyramid of needs calls human *needs of self actualization* (Maslow, 1943) related to morality, creativity and as such with inner peace and peace of the conscience. For instance, the rights to freedom of thought, conscience,

---

[37] Peace is at the same time a value, an end, and an asset to law. Peace is a value in which law engages in the issues of social coexistence through justice. [...] The peace that law is specifically interested in is the social peace, the peace of human society as a community (and not the personal inner peace or peace of conscience). (Barraca Mairal, 2005: 133).Translated by the author.

religion, opinion and expression[38] are a legal response to the human desire to meet needs of self-actualization (Maslow, 1943). All rights can be related to human needs at all levels of Maslow's pyramid of needs. Following Maslow (1943) and Rosenberg (2003) all humans may share some core human needs but we may also have very different ways of meeting those needs. In this sense, the judicialization of rights, for instance, is confronted with the need of materialization by relating them to inner dimensions of peace as well, and not merely to abstract notions.

2.3.1 Social Peace vs. Inner Peace?

Modern understandings of peace create a clear cut between peace as social contract and peace as embodied or spiritual experience. I discussed above how legal institutions seem to center the scope of action of the law only the contractual sphere. Now I want to deepen the discussion and explore the connection between rights and inner peace, and between inner peace and social peace. The 14th Dalai Lama in his Nobel peace prize lecture said:

> Peace […] starts with each one of us. When we have inner peace, we can be at peace with those around us. When our community is in a state of peace, it can share that peace with neighboring communities, and so on. […] What is important is that we each make a sincere effort to take seriously our responsibility for each other and for the natural environment we live in. (Gyatso -14 Dalai lama-, 1988)

When traditional legal doctrine addresses the issue of peace, it makes a separation between *personal/inner* peace and *social* peace of the community, making clear that legal norms refer specifically to human conduct that affect *social peace,* leaving any matters of inner peace aside to the domain of other type of rules, which appear to be less 'objective' or 'reasonable' and thus nearer to the unattainable *spiritual* field: *religious* and *moral* rules.

Via the spectrum of content of legal norms, namely *mandates, permissions, prohibitions and sanctions* (Alessandri and others, 1998: 26), legal norms attempt to address only human actions that 'objectively' cause unjustified damage to others. Nonetheless, when facing the complexity of human relations it seems like the inner and social fields are not so clearly separated. As mentioned in the former chapter, the transrational interpretation of peace

[38] See articles 18 and 19 Universal Declaration of Human Rights (1948)

approaches the *individual* not as that ultimate unit, which cannot be divided and is separate from others (Koppensteiner, 2009).

Then it is worth to bring up a reflection: is inner peace really disconnected from social peace and vice versa? Or do they influence each other? Does it mean that activities that are legally regulated do not influence personal experiences of peace? Does it mean that someone's inner peace does not contribute to social peace? As mentioned earlier, physicists and psychologists have developed consistent theories regarding interconnectedness of phenomena and persons concluding that we influence the environment around us and it influences us. In this sense, the energetic approach to peace explained by Dietrich (2008) should not be disconnected from the legal theory and practice. It is necessary to integrate a plurality of peaces to the legal practice if aiming to reduce violence in societies so turbulent and diverse such as the Colombian.

The discourse of human rights ultimately aims to 'secure' the inner peace of individuals via the establishment of different freedoms, from where persons are to be able to *open* to their potentials and capabilities instead of repressing them in what Galtung (1996) has called "positive peace." Issues of relevance for inner peace of the person are interconnected to dynamics of social peace and violence (direct-structural-cultural) so, the language of needs ought to be open to jurists with creativity, interpreted in each specific case and used accordingly.

Social peace as an absolute/perfect situation does not exist in the here and now, but refers to an ideal status that may be achieved in the future, a desire, something that is everything but our everyday life (Muñoz, 2006). The idea of all humans sharing the same values and points of view with no conflicts of interest whatsoever is not realistic. However, besides losing hope in any chance of finding joy in the present, there is also the option to embrace real life and real peace(s) as imperfect (Muñoz, 2006), contextual and relative, as a path more than a target. Actually, creativity and transformation can be seen as the core of an affirmative life and they are born exactly out of the dance between opposites, meaning, out of conflict (Koppensteiner, 2009: 92-101).

Social psychologist Philip Zimbardo (2008) explains the connection between inner peace, inner frustration, and peace and violence of societies. The author elaborates on how 'good/normal' people under the influence of systems of structural and cultural violence generally end up either using direct violence for survival or becoming part of those sophisticated systems after finding them very hard to resist.

Within such systems, those who end up using direct violence are categorized as 'bad apples' whose labeling and posterior separation, isolation or elimination is then justified by rational means, i.e. legally justified. Zimbardo suggests that the line separating good from evil is so thin that we all are equally susceptible to perform them both. After conducting research in humans exposed to simulated and real prison environments, both in roles of prisoners and guards, Zimbardo's findings suggest that violent social structures produce violent people and not the other way around (Zimbardo, 2008).

Hanna Arendt coined the *banality of evil* to refer to this phenomenon (Arendt, 2006). Her insight is that the great evils in history generally, and the Holocaust in particular, were not executed by extreme evil people but rather by ordinary people who accepted the state's premises and therefore participated with the view that their actions were normal. Arendt explains how structural dynamics that accept violence as means for peace reproduce violence and suffering loses its meaning; it becomes normal, accepted, part of the system. One does not have to be demonic, sadistic, or immanently cruel to contribute to a plethora of suffering. The majority of evil resides in the cult of simplicity, it consists of everyday conformity and order within a community or society (Arendt, 2006). Hence she alerts the need to be aware of the banality of evil and act to avoid its occurrence. Arendt's is a remarkably simple explanation of structural violence in Colombia via public policies of security enforced by the law.

2.3.2 Legal Education as Training for Hierarchy

The link between law and modernism can be also made by connecting Deleuze and Guattari's metaphor of horizontal *rhizomes* and hierarchical *arborecent* units (Deleuze & Guattari, 2004) with Duncan Kennedy's[39] article *'Legal Education as Training for Hierarchy'* (Kennedy, 1990) which later came to form part of the book *Legal Education as Reproduction of Hierarchy* (Kennedy & Carrington, 2004).

Similar to Deleuze and Guattari's argument, Kennedy analyses social power structures relating legal education and practice to "the endless attention to trees at the expense of forests" (Kennedy, 1990: 54). Following Kennedy's argumentation, I will connect some basic characteristics of legal education and practice with the *modern* worldview to see how some legal practices contribute to feeding cultures of structural and cultural violence. Part of

[39] US American Jurist from the school of Critical Legal Studies (CLS). Born in 1942, current professor of law at Harvard University.

the training for hierarchy within law studies begins with the narrative of an essential separation of respectable and not so respectable members of society and in feeding the stereotype of what it means to be identified as a lawyer. Kennedy (1990: 55) criticizes how many of the students "whose parents were not members of the professional/technical intelligentsia seem to feel that going to law school is an advantage in terms of the family history." It is rare for parents to actively disapprove of their children going to law school, "taking this particular step has a social meaning and that social meaning is success" (Kennedy, 1990: 55).

Kennedy's analysis is produced in the context of the US American legal culture, which diverges from the Colombian in many aspects, but taking into account the distance, I find his analysis at some extent similar to my own experience as a law student and, for a short period, legal practitioner in Colombia, thus I approach them as a significant contribution in the reflection of how jurists influence peace and violence through their work.

There are many legal practices silently building up the discourse of separation present already in the law classroom. The author observes that "the classroom experience sustains rather than dissipates ambivalence," based on facts such as "teachers being overwhelmingly white, male and deafeningly straight and middle class in manner" (Kennedy, 1990: 56). What takes place in the classroom is "pseudo-participation, [which] makes one intensely aware of how everyone else is doing, providing endless bases for comparison" (Kennedy, 1990: 56).[40]

One more point of connection between law and modernity is the narrative of disconnection of two human aspects: reason (Apollonian) and feelings (Dionysian). In law for example, this disconnection can be identified in the notions of order and care for the self and others, where the role of good protagonist is given to reason/order. "In most law schools, it turns out that the tougher, less policy-oriented teachers are the more popular" (Kennedy, 1990: 57), which reveals the pressure put against jurists and litigants to develop high technical expertise to handle normative systems and not so much interest in understanding social conflicts.

Dionysius is the antagonist in the 'successful lawyer' play. For example, showing emotions, or including reference to feelings in trials or lawsuits seems to have a very negative connotation, furthermore, changing perspec-

---

[40] For further analysis on the connections between comparisosns and violence see Rosenberg (2003), for whom comparisons are violent elements of communication given that they constitute a form of judgment that blocks compassion for the self and others.

tive on a concrete topic is a sign of not being a rigorous professional, you must show strong thinking (Vattimo, 2006) if you want professional success. These phenomena are curious considering that law is about dealing with human needs and social relations, a field that is especially close to the emotional human component. Logical schemes of argumentation are very useful in legal practice especially in the task of *judging*, but never *sufficient* (Atienza, 1999); however, often it simply takes over the emotional aspect, contributing to what Dietrich (2006a) addresses as the suppression of the Dionysian and its contribution to structures of violence.

When examining the study of so-called *cold* and *hot cases* in the classroom, Kennedy refers to this separation of the rational and the emotional aspects and their influence in hierarchical structures. *Cold cases* are those of "no political or moral or emotional significance" (Kennedy, 1990: 57), they have an intellectual content which "seems to consist of learning rules —what they are and why they have to be the way they are — while rooting for the occasional judge who seems willing to make them marginally more humane" (Kennedy, 1990: 57). This kind of case challenges students' rational abilities.

Hot cases on the other side are those involving "a sympathetic plaintiff — say, an Appalachian farm family— and an unsympathetic defendant —say, a coal company" (Kennedy, 1990: 57), which does not consider the needs of the family and whose aims are mere economic profits. With this kind of case, the point of discussion in class would be that emotional reactions or the expression of feelings of annoyance are "naive, non-legal, irrelevant to what you're supposed to be learning" (Kennedy, 1990: 58).

The cold case is boring, but you have to do it if you want your title as lawyer. "The hot case cries out for response, seems to say that if you can't respond you've already sold out; but the system tells you to put away childish things, and your reaction to the hot case is one of them" (Kennedy, 1990: 58). Without any intellectual resources in the way of knowledge of the legal system it will seem like emoting will only isolate and incapacitate you. The choice is to develop some calluses and hit the books, or admit failure almost before you have begun (Kennedy, 1990: 58).

The disconnection of the rational and the emotional human components in legal studies goes hand in hand with the separation of two aspects of analysis in the legal theory and practice: *pure legal technique* and *policy oriented analysis* (Kennedy 1990, 2002). When dealing with cold cases, students can exercise legal logic. These cases can be *wrongly decided* when not following the inner logic of the area (Kennedy, 1990). There are also cutting-edge cases, which the teacher sees as raising policy issues about growth or change in the law. Here we are dealing with "value judgments that have political overtones" (1990: 61). In this context, student's comments are not judged in terms of right and wrong anymore, "all student comments get pluralistic acceptance, and the teacher will reveal himself or herself to be either a liberal or a conservative rather than merely a legal technician" (Kennedy, 1990: 61).

Kennedy points out how the curriculum as a whole follows the hierarchical design according to which the ground rules of late-nineteenth-century laissez-faire capitalism are on top: contracts, torts, property, criminal law, and civil procedure, which are "taught as though they had an inner logic, as an exercise in legal reasoning, with policy [...] playing a relatively minor role" (Kennedy, 1990: 61). Additionally, the narrative of *universal individual rights* built up within the modern understanding of all humans aiming to the same *one peace,* locates the practice of law in the context of modernity, making it difficult to deal with tasks of creatively balancing contradictory rights and opening up for pluralism, because they challenge the legal logic. In this vein, Kennedy comments that rights' discourse is traditionally individualist and "willfully blind to the realities of *substantive* inequality" and as such the "rights discourse is a trap" (Kennedy, 1990: 62).

The training for hierarchy and rejection to difference finally takes place in law faculties with the silent message of what the profile of a successful lawyer looks like: typically white, hopefully heterosexual, in rational control of emotions, rigorous, middle class and with certain forms of talking, moving and living. In addition, there is an almost ignored fact: the grading system, which is based in comparison between students and narratives of individual failure or success with little constructive feedback and reflection on how the educational system is working as a whole. "Students internalize this message about themselves and about the world, and so prepare themselves for all the hierarchies to follow" (Kennedy, 1990: 64). This is how Kennedy argues that legal education causes and reproduces hierarchy, which is connected to modernity as worldview, in the sense that it creates stereotypes and fuels discrimination (Galtung, 1990).

I find this analysis of high relevance for the study of structural violence and the role of every one of us in it. However I do not believe that jurists are condemned to follow these patterns; that being a jurist *has to be* synonymous with violent practices. There is much room for creativity and cultures of peaces also within legal contexts; because creating norms and filling them with meaning are human actions. With *all* our human potential we create, use, criticize and transform the law. My argument here is that legal studies need to integrate peace studies; jurists' awareness of the many interpretations of peace in history and culture is essential to legal practices that facilitate positive peace.

Law transforms when people transform. Thus, the importance I give to Kennedy's arguments on hierarchy (1990) in hand with Arendt's *banality of evil* (2006) focuses on the importance of observing and permanently reflecting upon the influence of legal practices on the creation and reproduction of direct, structural and cultural violence (Galtung, 1990, 1996) so that legal practitioners are able to react to violence with responsibility instead of adding to its banality. Transrational approaches to peace, as suggested by Dietrich (2008), are not to reject modernity or humans' rational aspect as a whole, but to integrate it with the emotional capabilities that happen to be suppressed by modern narratives.

Conclusion

Law is a set of regulations of human conduct expressed in bilateral and coactive rules whose creation and use aim to the achievement of abstract values such as peace, order and justice. The concrete content of those values vary from one person or group to the other and transforms over time. Along history and school of thought, law has been interpreted in contrasting ways, while some authors see it as a tool to keep order and equilibrium in social relations others see it as a tool for social domination.

Iusnaturalism and Iuspositivism are classic perspectives on law; they define the law by focusing attention on the relation between norms and justice, who is entitled to define what is just and unjust and what defines the validity of norms. Contemporary legal researchers have analyzed law from other points of view; Tamanaha (2004) for instance refers to law as a tool to prevent tyranny. According to him the law limits the government's exercise of power, brings predictability to some social relations and controls abuses of power by the idea of 'the rule of law, not of persons'. He argues that there is no universal recipe on how to avoid tyranny; each community sets its own rules according to their vernacular values and model of relations.

Knowing which are the actual legal rules to be followed is not an easy matter since legal systems function in different ways. Some legal cultures are based on written rules and others on judges' rulings. Given the permanent transformation of legal practices both ways can become mixed and confused within one system. In this context, legal scholars have identified that the actual laws to follow can be: (1) what written rules say, (2) what judges say, (3) what legal principles say and (4) what comes out of processes of argumentation. All these dimensions can interplay in one legal case.

National law rests on the existence of the Hobbesian nation-state, which is built on the precepts of the absolute power of a strong state. Following Dietrich's (2008) variations on peace, within the national frame law aims for a modern peace, is based on a fundamental separation of correct/legal and incorrect/illegal people and behaviors and as such, it is an institution that fosters structural violence. Nonetheless, law is understood to exist in more contexts than the national, for instance native communities use coactive norms as a tool for organization.

The legal theory and practices are traversed by the concept of peace. Legal institutions are born out of the search for ordered-harmonious social relations. Given the essential role of peace for the law and following Atienza's (1999) idea on law as a process of argumentation and linguistic exchange, it is possible to conclude that plural interpretations of peace have an effect on the way norms, and concretely, rights, are argued and used.

3. Plural Peaces vs. Universal Human Rights

War tends to assimilate cultures to each other, whereas peace is that state in which each culture blooms in its own unique way. (Illich, 2006: 116.

Introduction

In the last chapter I argued that the use and interpretation of legal norms are influenced by variations on the concept of peace. Following this line, the human rights' discourse is shaped by energetic, moral, modern, postmodern and transrational perspectives of peace as well.

When persons or groups are considered 'national enemies,' as happens in Colombia in the context of the security policy, they are denied their humanity by the use of modern narratives, after which their *human* rights do not have to be respected any longer. With regard to my research question —*in the case of conscientious objection to military service in Colombia, how does the interpretation of the right to freedom of conscience vary according to Dietrich's five cultural variations of peace—*, in this chapter I will analyze how the modern interpretation expressed in the idea of *one/national peace* shapes an instrumental and exclusive understanding of *human dignity* and, consequently, fosters discriminatory interpretations of human rights.

This analysis will allow me to narrow the critique to the modern-legal type of peace to the concrete case of Human Rights Law and move on to the argumentation of objections to military service in Colombia, where the right to freedom of conscience of Colombian draftees was argued as a right to have concrete understandings of peace that diverge from perspectives besides the abstract-national peace.

3.1 Human Dignity and Denial of Full Humanity

3.1.1 Dehumanization and Pseudo-speciation

Human Rights' charters are considered to be one key achievement of humanity in the attempt for reducing domination and suffering. Human rights seek to establish and enforce the equal dignity of all humans. It is a response to practices of 'ranking' some people as better deservers of privileges and entitlements to fully develop the own potentials and abilities. Following Galtung (1996), it means neglecting positive peace for those who are discriminated against.

Following up on the idea of equal dignity, Bernard and others (2003) argue that when it comes to killing or harming a person, the offender tries to *de-humanize* the victim in order to feel less regret for the act of causing damage to a fellow human, to another of the same kind. According to biographer Lawrence J. Friedman (2000) it was Erik Erikson (1995) who coined the term *pseudo-speciation* in 1966 to refer to this phenomenon. On pseudo-speciation, Strozier & Flynn (1996) explain that:

> [Hu]mankind, while one species, has divided itself throughout its history — territorially, culturally, politically— into various groupings that permit their memories at decisive times, to consider themselves, more or less consciously and explicitly, the only true human species, and all others as less than human. (Strozier & Flynn, 1996: 51)

3.1.2 Indifference towards Death

Judith Butler (2006) explains how the life of *dehumanized* humans does not even *deserve* mourning, since it implies knowing what one has lost, respect and some sort of melancholia. Butler argues that people considered less human are not really known in their full humanity but are a mere target of exploitation, deprivation and violence, therefore their elimination is seen as normal, inevitable, deserved and justified (Butler, 2006). The identification of humans with a singular aspect of their lives such as belonging to a certain nation, social class, having a certain political opinion, gender, sexual orientation, profession or a certain religion, amongst others, has inspired many narratives of the *worthless human* (Butler, 2006).

Butler's (2006) link between dynamics of dehumanization and mourning can be observed in Colombia in the context of the armed conflict currently taking place between state and non-state armed forces (i.e. the state armed forces, paramilitaries, guerrillas and urban bands of organized crime). For example, when the government executes illegal group members during military operations, images of their corpses are displayed by mass media provoking pride in the armed forces and 'national' celebration. Notably, there are forbidden and hidden processes of mourning in Colombia, since the bodies of the 'illegal' are not related to human beings but to anti-values (Posada & Álvarez, 2010). Mourning 'their' death has become suspicious and politically incorrect. On indifference towards death in the aftermath of the Nazi Holocaust, Arendt said:

> *Por todas partes llama la atención que no haya reacción a lo sucedido [...]. La indiferencia con que se mueven entre los escombros encuentra su correspondencia en que nadie llora a los muertos.*[41] (Arendt, 2005: 302)

The authoritative identification of humans is characteristic of modernity and its rational discourses of separation based on: mental illness/inability to adapt (Zimbardo, 2008), security threats (Echavarría, 2010) and individual ability to achieve social status (Kennedy, 1990), among other dichotomies. All these radical identifications take people as individuals who are fundamentally wrong or evil (Zimbardo, 2008) without any consideration of wider social systems generating frustration and difficulty to meet needs (Rosenberg, 2003), thus structural and cultural violence (Galtung, 1996).

Erikson's *pseudo-speciation* (Erikson in Friedman, 2000) along with Rosenberg's (2003) *language of needs* show that some persons or groups are considered to deserve the *privilege* of having their needs met more than others do. The needs of 'dehumanized humans' seem not to be appreciated as *human* needs since they are defined by narratives of the wrong, abnormal, incorrect, evil and inconvenient or, in the language of law, the illegal. Those suppositions are fed by cultural means: political ideologies, religion, language, arts, and academia, in what Galtung calls *stereotyping* the other in the context of cultural violence (Galtung, 1990).

Language is a powerful tool used in processes of dehumanization. For instance, the use of numbers instead of names to identify people in prison, while, on account of the significance that names have for the dignity and uniqueness of the person, having a name is actually a human right.[42] Constructing images of the 'evil other' makes their elimination easier. Besides replacing names for numbers also nouns and adjectives play an important role: if a *category* such as 'terrorist', 'criminal', 'prostitute', 'dangerous migrant', or 'bad soldier' is killed it has a different social impact than killing a 'person' or a 'human' who has a name, a story, feelings, potentials, capabilities, emotions and shadows. The execution of the first type of person is often

---

[41] "Everywhere it is noteworthy that there is just no reaction towards what happened [...] The indifference with which people move among the debris finds its correspondence in the fact that no one mourns the dead" (Arendt, 2005: 302). Translation by the author.

[42] Article 7, Convention on the Rights of the Child: "The child shall be registered immediately after birth and shall have the right from birth to a name [...]." (Convention on the Rights of the Child, 1989: Article 7)

perceived as the triumph of criminal justice (justified-legal) while the execution of the second one is a crime (unjustified-illegal).

3.2 Pseudo-speciation by use of Language in Colombia

Dynamics of dehumanization by the use of language, coined by Galtung (1996) as cultural violence, can be clearly observed in Colombia. For instance, on 23 September 2010 the Colombian Army executed Víctor Julio Suárez Rojas, alias 'Mono Jojoy', leader of military operations of the Colombian guerrilla group FARC, together with around 20 other members of that non-state armed group. Remarkable nouns and pejorative adjectives were used to inform the news: Colombian president Juan Manuel Santos announced the guerrilla leader's death as "the fall of the symbol of terror" and the military operation was called '*Sodoma*' (Operation Sodom) (El Espectador, 2010).

Along with information on the military operation, *El Tiempo* newspaper published an article gathering people's opinions about the military operation, all of them referred to the deaths occurred in Operation Sodom as positive, *important for national peace* and —as Butler (2006) particularizes— justified and deserved (El Tiempo, 2010b).

Political magazine *Semana* published explicit full size pictures of the FARC leader's dead body, and referred to him as '*el coco*'[43] (Semana, 2010). Most Colombian newspapers displayed pictures of the wounded corpse. Most of the readers' online comments on the articles expressed delight and national pride. After the event, the Minister of Defense publicly stated:

> *Señor presidente* [in reference to ex-president Alvaro Uribe], *la consigna dispuesta por usted sigue siendo "Arreciar, Arreciar y Arreciar", y creo presidente que es un día de gloria, es un día de júbilo para los colombianos, y por supuesto le damos gracias a Dios porque nos ha bendecido con victoria, y damos gracias a nuestras Fuerzas Militares y de Policía por un trabajo sin celos, por un trabajo conjunto y coordinado, por un trabajo de alta precisión en combates muy intensos.*[44] (Rivera quoted in Ministerio de Defensa Nacional - República de Colombia, 2010)

---

[43] Monstrous imaginary figure used popularly in Latin America when threatening children. Its equivalent in the English language is the 'boogeyman.'

[44] "Mr. President, the slogan that you have stated continues to be "raging, raging and raging" against the enemy. It is a day of glory, a day of joy for Colombians. We thank God for bles-

On their part, the FARC informed the news also by using dehumanizing terms to refer to the Colombian President Santos, such as 'chucky', 'evil doll', and 'hyena', and to the Colombian government as 'oligarchic' and 'terrorist' (Anncol, 2010). Remarkably, while dehumanizing adjectives, and barely names, were used by the Government and the FARC, during the same day a name and glorifying adjectives were used from title to bottom line to inform the death of an anti-explosives dog used by the army during operation Sodom. The headline used was "*Sacha, un soldado irremplazable*" (Sacha, an irreplaceable soldier) (El Colombiano, 2010). No picture of the dogs' wounded body was published but pictures taken when it was alive.

After operation Sodom, the Colombian Minister of defense Rodrigo Rivera, sent a message to FARC's top leader, Alfonso Cano, warning him to surrender "in order to guarantee his right to life and be ensured dignifying treatment, like all members of the FARC under the condition that they decide to demobilize" (El Espectador, 2010).

The use of language to dehumanize the 'other' or the 'enemy' in Colombia implies an understanding of human dignity based not merely on the fact of being a human, but on special qualifications, i.e. being a *good* human, whatever it means according to the interpreter. This is how members of non-state armed groups in Colombia, which numbers arise to tens of thousands, are not qualified enough to enjoy human dignity; they do not deserve being treated with "equal concern and respect" as Dworkin (1977: 272) defines dignity.

3.3 Rights: Rejection of Pseudo-Speciation Narratives

Human rights declarations promulgated during the second half of the twentieth century in Europe and North America could be interpreted as an *articulated* social rejection against narratives of *pseudo-speciation.* In that sense they are a breakthrough in the history of human political relations.

sing us with victory and thank our military and police forces for a well executed joint and coordinated work, for the work of high precision that took place during very intense fighting" (Ministerio de Defensa Nacional - Republica de Colombia, 2010). Translation by the author.

It does not mean that collective awareness of human dignity did not exist before in other times and places. In this regard Dietrich (2000) explains that cultures have their own means to articulate their interest for human dignity and the *legal written* way (that characterizes Human Rights covenants) happens to be the prevalent form concretely in European and North American cultures in the second half of the twentieth century. The roots of the belief that everyone by virtue of their humanity is entitled to the respect of their human rights "lies in earlier tradition and documents of many cultures; it took the catalyst of World War II to propel human rights onto the global stage" (Human Rights Educators' Network, Amnesty International USA, 1998). Furthermore:

> Throughout much of history, people acquired rights and responsibilities through their membership in a group – a family, indigenous nation, religion, class, community, or state. Most societies have had traditions similar to the "golden rule" of "Do unto others as you would have them do unto you." The Hindu Vedas, the Babylonian Code of Hammurabi, the Bible, the Quran (Koran), and the Analects of Confucius are five of the oldest written sources which address questions of people's duties, rights, and responsibilities.
>
> In addition, the Inca and Aztec codes of conduct and justice and an Iroquois Constitution were Native American sources that existed well before the 18th century. In fact, all societies, whether in oral or written tradition, have had systems of propriety and justice as well as ways of tending to the health and welfare of their members. (Human Rights Educators' Network, Amnesty International USA, 1998)

Nonetheless, the importance of being aware of systematic dehumanization, and the realization of an equal consideration of everyone's needs as requisite for any idea of peace, became articulated in modern European societies after the intense suffering experienced during World War II when radical pseudo-speciation justified the extermination of 'inferior' people and violence was established as the only way out of the conflict, by both the Nazis and the allies.

Besides critical examples of social exclusion as political strategy, such as the Nazi Holocaust in Europe, the Rwandan genocide or South Africa's Apartheid, many other acts of violence take place every day based on modern narratives of the *worthless human,* meaning a consideration of the *other* and *otherness* as fundamentally wrong or inferior.

One example is the use of violence in Colombia out of discursive identities of a 'dangerous' or 'evil' other. The diverse, multicultural and multiethnic profile of the Colombian population has turned out to be a self-destruction weapon due to an extreme radicalization of cultural, ethnic and following Echavarría (2010) radical political identities. Stereotypes (Galtung,

1990) are being constructed according to differences of all kinds, for the case studies in this book, especially for differences in political opinion. There is an accepted discourse of justified use of violence.

The recognition of full humanity to all humans —no exception— was conceptualized and normalized as *Dignity,* the key concept behind all human rights. As such, it was included in the preamble of the Universal Declaration of Human Rights (UDHR):

> Whereas recognition of the inherent dignity and of the equal and inalienable rights of all members of the human family is the foundation of freedom, justice and peace in the world [...], therefore the General Assembly proclaims this Universal Declaration of Human Rights. (Universal Declaration of Human Rights, 1948)

This preamble is complemented with more references to Human Dignity in Articles 1 and 2, stating that "all human beings are born free and equal in dignity and rights" and "everyone is entitled to all the rights and freedoms [...] without distinction of any kind, such as race, color, sex, language, religion, political or other opinion, national or social origin, property, birth or other status" (Universal Declaration of Human Rights, 1948: Article 2).

The articulated awareness of the equal value of all humans regardless of our differences related to the postmodern idea of respect for otherness, non-discrimination and appreciation of *uniqueness*. Nonetheless, the posterior *enforcement* of human dignity —materialized in specific limits to tyranny in the form of specific *rights-obligations* (Tamanaha, 2004)— can also, in other contexts, signify an "imposition of universalism and uniformity" coming only from the north Atlantic perception of human dignity and disregarding the rest (Dietrich, 2000: 1).

3.4 Universal Human Good?

Tamanaha (2004) analyses the way in which many scholars consider the rule of law as a "universal human good." Since it helps *limiting governments in their exercise of power,* including a limitation for law making, the rule of law hence helps to prevent tyranny. "Preventing government tyranny was a concern in ancient Athens, a concern throughout the Medieval period, and continues to be a concern everyday today" (Tamanaha, 2004: 139). The nature of those limitations will vary from one society to the other but the need for limitations "will never be obsolete" (Tamanaha, 2004: 139). In this regard Tamanaha agrees that, since there is a need for controlling those in power in almost all societies, law is indeed a universal human good.

Nonetheless, he criticizes *universalism* concretely when legal limits to governments, let us say positive law and bills of rights, are transplanted from one society to the other. Tamanaha argues that each society has its own prevailing views on which limits to institute to the exercise of power and how to do it, since the nature of limitations varies with cultural, political and economic arrangements. He brings the example of cultural differences among so-called *eastern* and *western* societies within the context of *universal* bills of rights:

> Leaders of some Asian societies have raised objections to western delivered bills of rights declarations and individualistic in orientation, contrary to their communitarian cultures […] these views cannot be dismissed outright. Cultures are indeed different and personal liberty, as much as the west takes it for granted, cannot be justified in universalist terms. (Tamanaha, 2004: 139)

However, the contextualization of human rights needs to go beyond the east/west division, because the language it uses is insufficient and confusing. It is insufficient because it adds to the creation of two radical identities, namely east and west, ignoring the richness of cultural variations of the human kind. Moreover, it is confusing because it uses geography terms when referring to cultural and economic differences. These variances can be better appreciated in the following illustrations.

Illustration I. Map of Advanced Economies

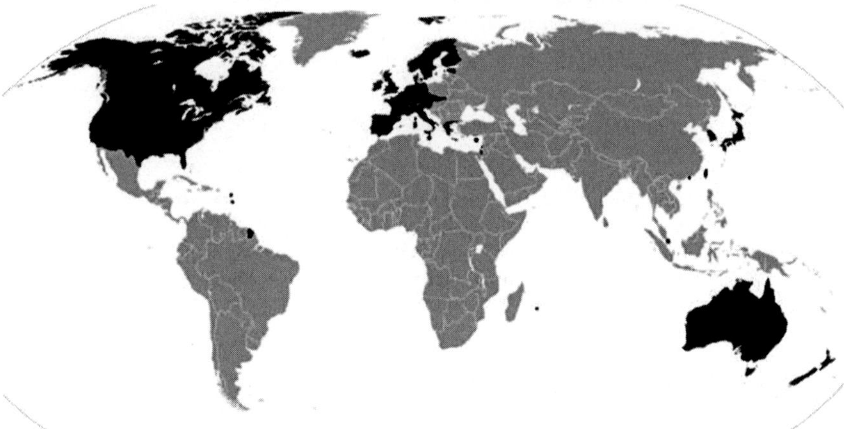

Advanced economies colored in black as classified by the International Monetary Fund (IMF, 2008). Other countries are in gray.[45]

Illustration II. Map of Civilizations

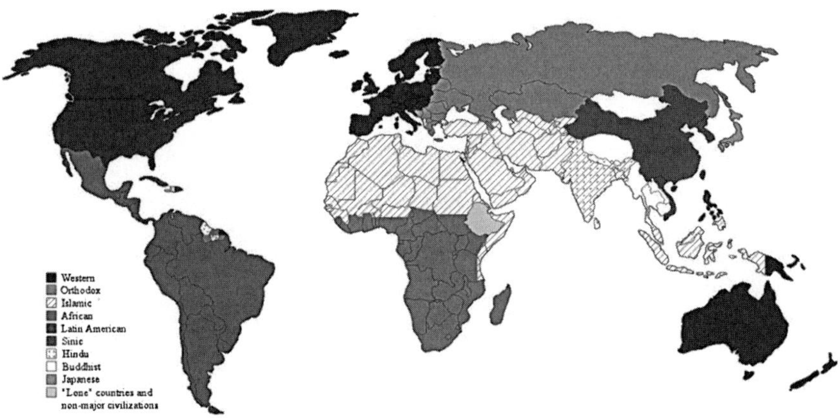

"The Many Faces of the Future: Why We'll Never Have a Universal Civilization" (Huntington, 1997: 76).

[45] For the latest database see *World Economic Outlook Database, April 2012* (IMF, 2012).

The selection of *developed* countries in Illustration I corresponds almost fully to the selection of *western* countries in Ilustration II, painted in black in both images. Notably, the term *west* is not used to referred to a geographical area but to developed countries. The term *developed* mostly denotes cultures characterized by strict scientific approaches to knowledge and economic models based on surplus-value of capital, in contrast to cultures based mostly on traditional approaches to knowledge and use of resources (Espinoza, 2001). According to this categorization, Latin America is not in the west and Australia is not in the East even though their geographical location speaks to the contrary.

Societies are diverse and in permanent movement; therefore it is possible to find traditional-ceremonial approaches in European and North-American communities as well as scientific-capitalist based sectors in Latin American, African, Japanese, Hindu, Sinic, Islamic and Orthodox contexts. The same applies to the diverse multicultural Colombian population. In this context, I argue that a conceptualization of plural Human Rights has to go beyond the east/west division acknowledged by Tamanaha (2004), because it reproduces static, dual categories, ignoring the multiplicity and concurrence of human (socio/legal) cultures. This is my argumentative basis for looking at pluralistic interpretations of Human Rights as an element for positive peace.

Conclusion

The modern understanding of peace is based on the exclusion of acts of deviation. Law as a tool for social order establishes which human conducts are to be excluded. The legal strategy is to exclude conducts via excluding the people who perform illegal conducts (using jail, death penalty or civil death). Human Rights' norms are a unique part of the law since they challenge the legal strategy of exclusion for peace.

All Human Rights' norms are founded upon the concept of human dignity. The term calls for the needs and suffering of all human beings to count equally. However, when the concept of human dignity is used within the frame of legal systems, the rights discourse can paradoxically be influenced by narratives of pseudo-speciation that *justify* exclusions in the name of an abstract peace, thus discrimination can becomes legal.

This is the case of the peace strategy based on security that has been taking place in Colombia since 2002. Dynamics of pseudo-speciation and dehumanization try to exclude people over their identification with certain groups. The model of national peace based on security designed in the 'democratic security policy' (Presidencia de la República y Ministerio de Defensa de Colombia, 2003) justifies that all people who fit or are suspected to fit 'deviated' identities deserve to lose their human dignity, therefore their human rights do not have to be respected any more. The critique of the universality of Human Rights from the perspective of Transrational Peaces focuses on the homogenization of human needs and ways of meeting them. For non-violent uses of the rights' discourse it becomes necessary to interpret rights as relative and relational.

4. PLURALITY OF PEACES IN LEGAL ACTION

What a sad wretched state of our political alternatives, though, that the nation becomes the only community imaginable, the only form of expressing social solidarity and escaping from individualism. (Hardt & Negri, 2009)

INTRODUCTION

In the previous chapters I argued that the philosophy of the many peaces needs to be integrated into the legal theory and practice since peace is an essential-traversal aspect to the law. I have circumscribed my analysis to Human Rights' norms and focused on the case of Colombia and its Democratic Security Policy in operation since 2002 (Presidencia de la República y Ministerio de Defensa de Colombia, 2003).[46]

The security policy uses law as one of its instruments; this is how the national peace based on exclusion of the 'deviant' has become a legal duty and expression of the Constitutional value of solidarity. The Colombian army has been given the mission to achieve the national peace by taking up arms against the 'enemy' in the context of internal armed conflict. This forced use of arms and the obligation to support the dehumanization of the 'enemy' has led many people to object to conscription.[47]

With reference to my research question —*In the case of conscientious objection to military service in Colombia, how does the legal argumentation of the right to freedom of conscience vary according to the five cultural variations of peace, i.e. energetic, moral, modern, postmodern and transrational peaces?*— in this chapter I will go through the constitutional case of objections to military service to be found in decision C-728/09. I will analyze how

---

[46] In 2010 Alvaro Uribe ended his period as president of Colombia and the government of new elected president Juan Manuel Santos introduced a new policiy called "Democratic Prosperity" including a security component called *Política Integral de Seguridad y Defensa para la Prosperidad* [Integral Security and Defense Policy for Prosperity]. See Ministerio de Defensa Nacional – República de Colombia. (2011). For further analysis see *De la seguridad democrática a la prosperidad democrática* (Pérez, 2010); *De la seguridad a la prosperidad democrática en medio del conflicto* (CODHES, 2011).

[47] Until October 2009 it was not legally possible to object to military service in Colombia.

arguments for the right to object military service are influenced by different interpretations of the concept of peace.

This chapter will be divided into two parts. In the first part I will go briefly through the meaning and story of conscientious objections and its relation to civil disobedience. Then I will analyze dynamics of pseudo-speciation in the concrete case of objectors to military service in Colombia followed by the examination of notions of *solidarity* expressed in the context of the nation-state. In the second part, I will study in detail the arguments in decision C-728/09 by contrasting them to Dietrich's variations on peace aiming to find out whether the argumentation of rights varied accordingly.

4.1 Conscientious Objections to Military Service

4.1.1 Origin and Meaning

Conscientious objections are a particular form of Civil Disobedience. The term 'civil disobedience' was coined by Henry David Thoreau in his 1848 essay to explain his refusal to pay the state poll tax implemented by the government of the United States to prosecute a war in Mexico and to enforce the Fugitive Slave Law (Brownlee, 2007, 2012).

In his essay, Thoreau (in Brownlee, 2007) maintains that some people are reformers, in the sense that they serve their society with their consciences; they try to change the status quo and for that reason are commonly treated by the state as enemies. Thoreau himself spent time in jail for his protest. Many after him have identified their protests as acts of civil disobedience and have been sent to prison (Thoreau, 1993; Brownlee, 2007, 2012).

In accordance to Rawls' widely recognized account of civil disobedience: "civil disobedience is a public, non-violent, conscientious yet political act, contrary to law usually done with the aim of bringing about a change in laws or policies of the government" (Rawls, 1971: 320). One important element of civil disobedience is *conscientiousness*, which points to the sincerity and conviction with which civil disobedients breach the law. For many disobedients, their breach of law is demanded of them not only by self-respect and moral consistency but also by their perception of the interests of their society. Through their disobedience, they draw attention to laws or policies that they believe require reassessment or rejection (Brownlee, 2007, 2012). In the context of plural peaces, civil disobedience can be interpreted as a clash amongst different perspectives of peace, given that one of them is enforced by law and the others consequently suppressed.

'Civil disobedience' is a general term used to refer to a breach of law for reasons of conscientious disagreement, but it can be displayed in a variety of forms very distinct from one another, such as conscientious objection, radical protest and revolutionary action (Thoreau, 1993; Brownlee, 2007). Conscientious objections are driven by ethical considerations that may assume different forms: religious, humanitarian, moral or philosophical (Falcón y Tella & Muckley, 2004) and are characterized by the objector's *fidelity to the legal system*, in contrast to other forms of disobedience that imply full denial of the legitimacy of institutions, as in the case of *militant protest* and *revolutionary collective disobedience*. In the case of legal objections, there is protest against specific duties by acting within the bonds of the law (Singer, 1973; Brownlee, 2007, 2012).

In regard to collective civil disobedience, there is a clear example of happening at the very moment that I am writing these lines. It is February 11, 2011 the day when Mr. Hosni Mubarak resigned from his position as president of Egypt after 30 years of dictatorship. Since 25 January 2010 people turned massively to the streets in Cairo and Alexandria waving a protest against the government, demanding a change of leader and a more participatory system of government. The massive protests led to the president's resignation and decision to call for elections. This is a clear example of an act of collective civil disobedience where legitimacy of public institutions is rejected altogether. Their act of disobedience has no place within the bonds of the Egyptian law since there is no right to demand a change of government system, neither a legal tool to realize it. In this regard Slavoj Žižek explains:

> From the start, the violence of the [Egyptian] protesters has been purely symbolic, an act of radical and collective civil disobedience. They suspended the authority of the state […]. When [the U.S.] President [Barack] Obama welcomed the uprising as a legitimate expression of opinion that needs to be acknowledged by the government, the confusion was total: the crowds in Cairo and Alexandria did not want their demands to be acknowledged by the government, they denied the very legitimacy of the government. (Žižek, 2011)

Distinctly, people who use conscientious objections as acts of civil disobedience differ from cases of collective civil disobedience in the sense that they accept the legitimacy of the rule of law and are willing to respect it. Given its place at the boundary of fidelity to law, it is said to fall between legal protest, on the one hand, and conscientious refusal, revolutionary action, militant protest and organized forcible resistance, on the other hand (Brownlee, 2007, 2012). Objectors accept the legitimacy of the law and may respect other people's compliance to it, but their particular context, background and value system makes them feel in deep contradiction towards its observance.

Following Rawls, Falcón y Tella & Muckley (2004) explain that conscientious objections are individual and do not appeal to the majority's sense of justice. The objector is rather interested in the peaceful resolution of his/her own personal dilemma. Yet various objectors can unite in their demands and transform their action into a collective protest movement aiming at wider political change. Most commonly used legal objections refer to the use of arms, paying taxes aimed at what they see as damaging purposes and medical practice of euthanasia, abortion and blood transfusions.

4.1.2 Colombian Conscription System

Military service in Colombia is mandatory for all males over the age of 18, for a period between 12 and 24 months. Serving in the military implies joining the army as a soldier or auxiliary police force in one of the following types: (1) *soldado regular* (private) serving between 18 and 24 months; (2) *soldado bachiller* (high school graduate soldier) for 12 months; (3) *soldado campesino* (peasant soldier) between 12 and 18 months and (4) *auxiliar de policía* (auxiliary police force) for 12 months (Law 48/1993: Article 13). It is not compulsory for women, who can join the army voluntarily. It is stated in law that it will be mandatory also for women "when circumstances of the country require so and the Government determines it" to serve in logistical, administrative, social, cultural and environmental tasks within the military (Law 48/1993: Article 10).

According to Law 48/1993, *all men* have the legal duty to *take up arms* when "necessary to defend the national independency and public institutions" (Law 48/1993: Article 3), both during military service and later as reservists. This obligation ends at the age of fifty (Article 10). Nonetheless, there are some legal exemptions regarding the general duty to take up arms. They distinguish between *peacetime* and *wartime.*[48]

There are two groups of men who are fully exempted from the military service. This exemption means at both 'peace and war times' and includes exemption from any future obligation as reservists. The groups are (1) men

[48] Despite the actual confrontation between state and non-state armed groups that is taking place in Colombia, officially the law establishes that there is peacetime. There is no official declaration of war because the government, in the frame of the security policy since 2002, decided to address non-state armed groups as 'common criminals' (terrorists) instead of political actors. Thus, many of the legal norms that are part of the security policy and should be exceptional (to be used only in wartime) are ordinary laws. The state of exception has become the rule.

with physical and sensorial disabilities, and (2) members of indigenous communities who live in their ancestral territories and keep indigenous social, cultural and economic integrity (Law 48/1993: Article 27).

Other groups can elude military service only during *peacetime*, under the condition of registering and paying a fee of military compensation (Law 48/1993: Article 28). Nevertheless they have future obligation as reservists in case of *wartime*. These groups are:

(1) The clergy and religious men with full dedication to their worship; (2) men who have been condemned to prison with the loss of political rights, until obtaining rehabilitation; (3) the only child, (4) the orphan who attends with his work the subsistence of siblings unable to earn a living; (5) the son of parents unable to work or over sixty years, when they have no income, pension or means of subsistence; (6) the brother or son of someone who has died or acquired any physical or mental detriment in acts of service; (7) married men; (8) men with legal inabilities; (9) the children of officers, non-commissioned officers and civil servants of the Armed Forces who have died or acquired a total and permanent disability in combat or in acts of service and for reasons inherent to it, unless they voluntarily want to join the Army (Law 48/1993: Article 28) and (10) since 2001, internally displaced people are granted a temporary (three-year validity) military certificate (Resolution 1879/01).

4.1.3 Jurisprudence before 2009

The legislation on conscription does not include conscientious objectors in the list of exempted from military service. Neither the Constitution includes a concrete right in this respect, so when young men object drafting for reasons of conscience, the army and judges respond negatively by arguing that Colombian law does not regulate objections to military service, thus they do not exist as a right (Constitutional Court in Decision T-409/92).

> *En Colombia tampoco es admisible esta posibilidad [objeción de conciencia al servicio militar], igualmente propuesta y rechazada en la Asamblea Nacional Constituyente [de 1991], de tal modo que no existe en nuestro Derecho Público norma alguna que haga lícita al individuo la conducta de negarse a tomar o a emplear las armas que le suministran las Fuerzas Militares para los fines que*

> *la Constitución Política indica.*[49] (Constitutional Court in Decision T-409/92:10)

This argument has been rejected by several sectors of the Colombian civil society that oppose the use of arms by principle, and hence consider the impossibility to object to military service as a violation of their fundamental right to freedom of conscience. As a result of such rejection, several claims of unconstitutionality against the conscription law were submitted to the Constitutional Court since 1992, but judges maintained their jurisprudence until 2009[50] by by means of two main elements: (1) the *historical argument,* and (2) an argumentation of the *principle of solidarity* strictly in the frame of the nation-state.

Historical Argument

According to the Constitutional Court (in Decision T-409/92), the Colombian nation has already decided to reject objections to military service in the past, therefore judges are not entitled to change that mandate in the present. A proposal regarding conscientious objections to military service was presented to the National Constituent Assembly back in 1991 when the Constitutional text was written and it was not approved by the Assembly as part of the Constitutional text. In this line of logic, the legal objection to military service is not a Constitutional right in Colombia because the National Constituent Assembly had decided so. As a consequence, the decision to exclude drafting objections from the national law was to be protected by the Constitutional Judges.

> *La garantía de la libertad de conciencia no necesariamente incluye la consagración positiva de la objeción de conciencia para prestar el servicio militar. [...] de allí que deba afirmarse la impracticabilidad de tal figura en cualquiera de sus modalidades en aquellos sistemas constitucionales que no la han consagrado, como acontece en el caso colombiano. Una propuesta en el*

---

[49] "In Colombia, this possibility [conscientious objection to military service] is not admissible, it was proposed to but rejected by the National Constituent Assembly, therefore there is no legal norm in our legal system that allows the individual to refuse taking up arms as part of the Armed Forces for the purposes that the Constitution states" (Constitutional Court in Decision T-409/92:10). Translation by the author.

[50] In 1992 (Decision T-409/92) the Constitutional Court first decided negatively on objections to military service. The argumentation used by the Court in 1992 was repeated in 1994, 1995 and 2001 to decide on new related claims brought by citizens (Decisions C-511/94; T-363/95; C-740/01). Such line of decision was valid until October 2009, when the Court changed its precedent in Decision C-728/09 (to be analyzed in chapter four).

> *sentido de introducirla expresamente en el texto de la Carta de 1991, presentada por el constituyente Fernando Carrillo fue negada por la Asamblea Nacional Constituyente, sin que pueda afirmarse que de los textos aprobados se deduzca siquiera un principio de objeción.*[51] (Constitutional Court in Decision T-409/92: 9)

This idea was rejected and challenged in the frame of a new constitutional claim in 2009 and will be discussed in detail in chapter four.

'National' Interpretation of the Principle of Solidarity

The second argument to maintain jurisprudence unfavorable to objections refers to the principle of solidarity. The Constitutional Court (in Decision T-409/92) held that military service is an expression of the legal principle of solidarity. "The duty of military service is based on the postulate that *collective interests* prevail over the individual's" (Constitutional Court in Decision T-409/92: 1). The Court argued that social relations in modern and contemporary states are based on a balance between rights and duties, where most duties refer to solidarity and the maintenance of basic principles necessary for living together (Constitutional Court in Decision T-409/92). In this sense, military service is an expression of solidarity aiming at national peace, "considering that the purpose of military service is the participation of the citizenry in the achievement and maintenance of peace" (Constitutional Court in Decision C-511/94: 23).

In this line of logic, constitutionally defined collective national interests such as sovereignty and integrity of the national territory were supreme interests that were to be defended by all Colombians as expressions of solidarity towards each other, even if the actions needed to undertake such protection compromise the life or rights of the person. My observation from the perspective of peace studies poses the following question: is the nation-state the only way to express solidarity?

The two former arguments along with the content of the right to freedom of conscience were subject to discussion in the frame of a new claim of unconstitutionality brought to the Colombian Constitutional Court in 2009 and

[51] "The right to freedom of conscience does not necessarily include a right to object to military service. [...] therefore such objections cannot be used in those constitutional systems that do not include them in their constitutions, as happens in the case of Colombia. One proposal to include objections to military service in the 1991 Constitution was introduced by constituent Fernando Carrillo and denied by the National Constituent Assembly. Hence it cannot be claimed that the text of the adopted constitutional text includes even a principle objection" (Constitutional Court in Decision T-409/92: 9). Translation by the author.

decided in decision C-728/09. More than 400 organizations from different cultural affiliations joined the discussion, presenting a multiplicity of perspectives on peace, solidarity and security in Colombia. This time the case decision was favorable to the petitioners, consequently the Court's precedent changed. The content of the lawsuit and legal process will be explained in detail in subchapter 4.1.7. Beforehand, I will present a short analysis on the problem of violation of rights that in turn generated the lawsuit.

4.1.4 The Violence involved in 'National Solidarity'

In the case of Colombia, the obligation of all men to "take up arms to defend national independency and public institutions" (Law 48/1993: Article 3) has been traditionally understood as deriving from the Constitutional principle of *solidarity*: "the duty of military service is based on the postulate that *collective interests* prevail over the individual's" (Constitutional Court in Decision T-409: 1; my emphasis). But then, what does solidarity mean within the context of this norm?

As a guiding concept, I will use Spinosa and others' (1999: 4) understanding of solidarity as "the ground of meaningful community." In order to understand the meaning and scope of solidarity in the case of obligatory military service in Colombia, I propose two questions: (1) what are those 'collective interests' prevailing over the individual's that are to be protected by young men who join the Colombian armed forces? And (2) what is the 'meaningful' aspect of the Colombian community that is to be protected by the armed forces?

The collective interests pursued by the national army are established in the following terms: "The armed forces will have as their primary purpose the defense of the sovereignty, independence, and integrity of the national territory and of the Constitutional order" (Constitution of Colombia, 1991: Article 217). This norm highlights elements of the nation-state, such as 'sovereignty', 'integrity of territory' and 'Constitutional order' as collective interests that every man in Colombia should be committed to defend; interests that should propel people to die and kill an the name of the nation (Anderson, 2006).

If solidarity recalls the ground of "meaningful community" (Spinosa and others, 1999) then the concrete *meaningfulness* given to the Colombian collective by the armed forces is based on a normative concept of the *nation*. This is how the act of taking up arms to physically exterminate those nationals and foreigners who are suspected of stepping outside 'sovereignty', 'integrity of the territory' or 'Constitutional order' is interpreted as an expression of solidarity. "According to the government 'we' can recognize 'them' because they do not act 'in solidarity' with the security effort" (Echavarría, 2010: x). "The concept that the government introduces for making the borders between 'us' (good citizens) and 'them' (terrorists) is the notion of 'patriotic solidarity' disguised as a Constitutional duty for all Colombians" (Echavarría, 2011: 7).

Limiting human solidarity to the mere sphere of the nation is a legal source of pseudo-speciation practices in Colombia. National solidarity uses the separator model 'us' (legal) vs. 'them' (illegal). Such categorization makes it possible to justify the loss of 'their' human dignity or right to have rights (Arendt, 1966) in the name of solidarity. In this way national solidarity is not a type of solidarity expressed towards humans but only towards those humans who comply with the national model of peace based on security. I contend that the rising rates of interpersonal violence in Colombia from 2002 to 2010 (CNP, 2010; INMLCF, 2009) or new culture of intolerance as it has been called (Semana, 2011a) are in part associated to dominant discourse on national solidarity that sustains the security policy (Presidencia de la República y Ministerio de Defensa de Colombia, 2003) and furthermore, informs the concept of dignity and interpretations of rights in violent ways.

Hardt and Negri (2009) expressed their dissatisfaction about the limits of mere national bonding. They pointed out that it is "a sad indication of the wretched state of our political alternatives, though, that the nation becomes the *only* community imaginable, the only form of expressing social solidarity and escaping from individualism" (Hardt & Negri, 2009: 163, my emphasis). If human solidarity is to count as means for peace in Colombia, it has to go beyond the limits of the nation, it has to widen up to find collective meaningfulness also in the fact of being different from each other.

Horowitz and Horowitz explain that Arendt, for instance, understands solidarity beyond the limits of the nation; she perceives it as the "only principle that refers directly to human suffering" (Horowitz & Horowitz, 2006: 142). Hansen (1993) expounds that Arendt's 'world of solidarity' is a world in which people can *be with* others, and neither for, nor against them; it overcomes the isolation of each individual and refers to 'togetherness'. For Arendt, without this togetherness there can be only *instrumental relations* between people, which ultimately rob them of their human dignity (Arendt in Hansen, 1993).

Following Hoelzl (2004), Echavarría (2011) explains how, in the frame of the Colombian security policy, solidarity does not connote *standing in for one another*, but "to be a member of a national body that sacrifices its life (biological and political) in the name of security for all" (Echavarría, 2011:

3). Elaborating upon Hoelzl's argumentation (2004), Echavarría (2011) says that the bedrock of acts of solidarity is *reciprocity*, hence, when someone is forced to give his/her own life for someone else, the question of asymmetrical solidarity arises. "The phenomenon of the sacrifice pushes this reciprocal understanding to its limits" (Hoelzl, 2004: 46).

This kind of group solidarity promotes Erikson's *pseudo-speciation* since "in the name of the group people become willing to discriminate, dehumanize and even kill, sometimes over smilingly minor differences" (Erikson in Hoover, 2004: 130). National solidarity is a value that fosters violence in Colombia, since it uses *national dignity* instead of *human dignity* to sustain itself. Part of the national dignity is to physically eliminate those endangering the nation. That task has been given to the Colombian army and has provoked many recruited men to object to military service and many jurists to look for ways change the conscription law. If solidarity is "limited to solidarity with 'friends', with those whom one agrees with (economically and politically), then it turns into a weapon of violence, exclusion and a tool to silence dissenting voices" (Echavarría, 2011: 14).

In this line, when criticizing the *securitized* notion of solidarity that means cohesion *against* 'the other' Echavarría (2011) proposes a more inclusive and hence challenging meaning of solidarity from a peace studies perspective: *solidarity with strangers*. The call is for "a new meaning of solidarity away from security and to remember that solidarity among all people necessarily implies going beyond standing in for one's friends and requires *standing in for strangers"* (Echavarría, 2011: 14).

4.1.5 Pseudo-speciation of Objectors

In view of the concept of *pseudo-speciation* mentioned in subsection 2.4.1, I propose that within the Colombian context of armed conflict, people who have perspectives of peace that diverge from the modern or that integrate the energetic perspective in the legal are victims of pseudo-speciation in Colombia.

From 2002 to 2010, under the presidency of Alvaro Uribe, a modern perspective of peace based on *security* was officially established as the public strategy to deal with the armed conflict in the country (Echavarría, 2010). Expressing opinions unfavorable to military operations in the context of the security policy leads to loss of rights, being objectors to military service one case. The security policy gravitates around the concept 'enemy'; consequently, alongside with the legal adjustments needed to undertake military operations at a bigger scale, there has been a discursive project of construction of the 'enemy' identity. In tune with the strategy adopted by the United States government after the attacks in New York on 11 September 2001, the Colombian government started to refuse the existence of an internal armed conflict with the presence of belligerent groups and started to officially call all opposing groups "terrorists" (Konrad-Adenauer-Stiftung. Oficina Colombia, 2008).

This public policy called 'Democratic Security Policy' accepts, legalizes and encourages the physical extermination of the 'enemy' as essential for the path to national peace. Such policy has led to the expenditure of an important portion of the public funds to finance militarization.[52] In this vein, the violent death of people identified in the category of 'enemy' instead of in the category of 'good Colombians' (Echavarría, 2010) is not legally considered homicide anymore, which allows the government to publicly present statistics of rising numbers of people executed by the army. Furthermore, soldiers who manage to kill more 'enemies' receive medals of honor and are given the political identity of 'national heroes'.[53]

The project of cultural construction of the 'enemy' identity leads people in Colombia to the necessary performance of political actions in every-day life. For instance, having a strong opinion about how important it is to physically exterminate the 'enemy' is seen as forming part of the 'group of good Colombians'. Furthermore, taking action into actually exterminating 'the enemy' is even better. In fact, it is stimulated by the state via payment of financial *rewards*, conformation of *networks of cooperation* and by strengthening the 'security-oriented' meaning of *solidarity*.[54] Conversely, not having a strong opinion about the physical extermination of the 'enemy' is considered support or identification with it.

Following Hall (1996) Echavarría points out that to occupy a category, "the subject has to invest in it. The subject must answer to the hailing of discourse and practices" (Echavarría, 2010: 123). "The subject categories produced by the in/security discourse in Colombia include the state, the sovereign people or nationals (the 'us') and the 'others' (terrorists, i.e. 'them'), as

---

[52] In 2010, Colombia was the Latin American country that allocated the most money to military spending in relation to its Gross Domestic Product (GDP) with 3.7 percent (Portafolio, 2010).

[53] In 2009 the Colombian army launched a campaign on television and radio called "Heroes in Colombia do exist" (Ejército Nacional de Colombia, 2009). The expression 'heroes' has been used by Colombian ex-president Alvaro Uribe to refer to members of the national army.

[54] For further information, see Cooperar para la Seguridad de Todos (Presidencia de la República y Ministerio de Defensa - Colombia, 2003: 60-62).

well as the markers that divide the good nationals from the bad/terrorist ones" (Echavarría, 2010: 123).

In regard to the case of objections to military service, not fulfilling the radical political identities enforced by security policies after 2002 has been a reason to exclude people with energetic-moral-postmodern and transrational approaches to peace (Dietrich, 2008) from the group of 'good Colombians', and, because there is no *in-between* (Muñoz, 2006), consequently placing them in the side of the 'enemy'. This is how any person who dares to invest in criticizing the violent means used by the state to *secure* national peace is immediately placed by "discursive formation" (Echavarría, 2010: 123) on the side of the 'others' or 'them'.[55]

Besides having to deal with the personal struggle to fit into radical discursive identification, conscientious objectors find themselves losing concrete rights. Following Law 48/1993, refusing military draft brings negative legal consequences for men, namely: impossibility to graduate from university, impossibility to access formal work opportunities and restricted mobility within the national territory (Law 48/1993: Articles 36-42). A group of anthropology students from Javeriana University and a group of conscientious objectors (in Decision C-728/09: 69-77)[56] commented that only people belonging to privileged economic classes could afford to pay the fee of military compensation in order to be excluded from military service in Colombia. Additionally, they argued, corruption is often used to get the army to receive the compensation fee even if the person does not meet any of the conditions established in Law 48/1993 to do so; therefore it is common to *buy* the military certification amongst people who can, "as it is well known, most of the victims of armed conflict in Colombia belong to the less privileged sectors, who in no case can exercise their rights" (Antropology students and objectors in Decision C-728/09: 76).

---

[55] An example occurred in February 2011 when the Colombian ex-president Alvaro Uribe placed Nobel Peace Prize Adolfo Perez Esquivel into the category of 'enemy' by publicly accusing him to be "serving Colombian terrorists" (Semana, 2011b). This discursive action took place in the context of a forum held in Argentina called "Foro por la paz en Colombia" after Perez Esquivel criticized violations of human rights in Colombia in the name of the security policy.

[56] The text of decision C-728/09 that corresponds to the page numbers I use for references in this book, is the word file uploaded in the official website of the Colombian Constitutional Court, available at http://www.corteconstitucional.gov.co/relatoria/2009/C-728-09.htm, last accessed 29 September 2012.

4.1.6 Need for Transformation: Why some Decide to Object in Colombia?

Military service is not a negative institution by itself, however, under some circumstances and for some persons it can be problematic rights-wise. In fact, I maintain that military service can be a positive learning experience; it can be a valuable opportunity for army members to reflect upon important issues such as responsibility, discipline, structure, teamwork, decision-making processes, and organized response to emergency situations. It is my understanding that under conditions of institutional respect for human dignity, joining the army can be a precious physical and mental training for draftees and professional army staff. Moreover, I consider that communities benefit from having an institution capable of giving immediate response to crisis situations of many kinds. However, while military service in Colombia can be a learning experience for some young men, it can be very destructive for others.

Joining the army can be destructive not only in terms of lives, considering the situation of armed conflict in Colombia, but also regarding convictions of conscience and ethics. Even if there is no open armed confrontation, armies are based on hierarchical structures of power and involve the use of weapons against contextually defined enemies, which responds to a modern interpretation of peace and security in the frame of the nation-state and may oppose resistance to other interpretations. This is how obligatory military service without the option to object constitutes a legal obligation to perform the modern model and a prohibition from assuming other perspectives of peace.

For many Colombians, joining the army means taking part in the armed conflict, which they may not want to do for ideological or life threatening reasons. An organization called Collective of Conscientious Objectors (*Acción Colectiva de Objetoras y Objetores de Conciencia, ACOOC*), submitted a concept to the Constitutional Court presenting reasons why people object to military service in the particular Colombian context. “Military service is a violation of the intimate convictions on non-violence in which we base our practices” (ACOOC in Decision C-728/09: 67). “We defend an attitude of respect for otherness and care for the other, of expressing sensitivity; we defend horizontal models of relations, solidarity, listening and non-violent approach to conflicts; all these elements make it irreconcilable for us to join a military institution” (ACOOC in Decision C-728/09: 67).

This organization of objectors expressed being convinced of the need to work for their country from a standpoint different from the armed one, that is the way they face the reality of a country still at war after six decades of armed confrontation aiming at peace with no sustainable solution (Decision C-728/09: 64). According to the ACOOC (in Decision C-728/09: 66-69), Colombian young people may object to military service for several reasons. One is having had traumatic experiences related to the armed conflict. In this regard, some young men refuse their participation in the official armed forces as well as in any of the illegal armies conformed by paramilitary or guerrilla groups within the Colombian territory. It is the case of men in a situation of displacement who were forced to move from rural areas to capital cities after suffering life threats for having refused recruitment by non-state armed groups. In the cities, they find themselves under the paradoxical situation of being recruited once again, this time by the state armed forces. Their reasons of conscience to refuse the use of arms are "not exclusive of one of the armed groups but of any armed institution that serves multiplying the armed conflict, including the national army" (ACOOC in Decision C-728/09: 67).

In other cases, men object to military service after being victims of state crimes, which motivates an ethical and even psychological impossibility to become part of the institution who acted as perpetrator in their cases (ACOOC in Decision C-728/09). For other objectors, the fact of having experienced episodes of violence in their families such as homicides and labor exploitation related to narcotraffic is determining to express objections to military service. For some people who have not been direct victims of the armed conflict, the fact of living in zones of high risk in the context of armed conflict creates aversion and radical opinions opposing armed solutions to conflict (ACOOC in Decision C-728/09: 67).

Some of the reasons to object to military service for conscientious dissent in Colombia are described by three testimonies of young people who found themselves caught in the legal impossibility of exercising their rights. These testimonies were collected in 2009 by a group of anthropology students from the Javeriana University in Bogotá,[57] along with a group of objectors to military service[58] (in Decision C-728/09: 69-77).

The first is the life story of Alvaro Alfonso Peña, a young man who was born in Bogotá in 1985:

> *Recuerdo que llegó en un momento en mi vida en el que sentía que no estaba haciendo mucho por mi vida ya que no tenía un empleo. [...] la única 'oportunidad' que se nos presenta a muchos jóvenes de los sectores populares es integrarse al Ejército Nacional de Colombia, el ejército vende el prestar servicio*

---

[57] Denise Ganitzky, Catalina Martínez Sarmiento, Ingrid Díaz and Juan Pablo Vera Lugo.
[58] Estefanía Gómez Vásquez, Julián Andrés Ovalle Fierro and Álvaro Alfonso Peña.

> *militar como una oportunidad laboral, social y una forma de adquirir oportunidades en nuestras vidas, y cómo no, si sin libreta no dan trabajo, ni puedes graduarte de tu carrera. [...]*
>
> *Esta era la única opción que se me presentaba, una opción que no quería tomar, sin embargo la ley me obliga a prestar servicio militar, sin tener en cuenta qué pienso, creo o qué quiero hacer con mi vida [...]. Sin embargo, sigo adelante siendo un objetor de conciencia que quiere construir una cultura no violenta en su país como estrategia para la disminución del contexto de militarización que se vive en Colombia.*[59] (Peña in Decision C-728/09: 70-71)

The second is the life story of Julián Ovalle, born in 1982. He narrates how the life of his family was negatively changed by the situation of militarization and explains his disagreement regarding the fee of military compensation:

> *Pagar un recibo de cuota de compensación militar era asumir una deuda muy alta por una institución que yo no reconocería como cercana, además implicaba sumar dinero a los cientos de miles de millones de pesos que se gastan en balas y bombas. El pago de la libreta implica una compensación por no poner mi cuerpo al servicio de la arbitrariedad y la muerte. Sobre todo, el pago de la libreta implicaba la imposibilidad de pagar una próxima matrícula universitaria. Por todo ello, aplacé indefinidamente el trámite con el propósito de pensar el proceso de ingreso a la universidad, lo cual era más relevante para lo que veía en mi vida.*
>
> *[...] Vivimos con mi familia las consecuencias de la desfasada lucha antisubversiva del ejército colombiano; en el año 2000 mi padre recibió cinco balas de las que hemos pagado los colombianos para nuestra seguridad. Por fortuna esas balas, que debían segar la vida de algún guerrillero lo hicieron sin gravedad un día que se dirigía a su casa después de un día de trabajo en el municipio de Albán, Cundinamarca. Algún joven asustado y armado que estaba esa noche en la carretera Panamericana por la obligatoriedad de participar en la guerra, o por un sueño de servicio a la patria, o como es muy frecuente, por una falta estructural de oportunidades educativas y laborales, disparó por error en defensa de su vida. Esos disparos desencadenaron la balacera que dejó 68 impactos de bala en la camioneta de mi padre, tal como lo arrojó la investigación de la justicia penal militar.*

---

[59] "I remember there came a time where I felt I was not doing much for my life since I did not have a job. [...] the only 'opportunity' for many young people from the popular sectors is to join the National Army of Colombia. The military sells military service as a job opportunity and a way to gain opportunities in our lives, and in fact it is the only way, given the fact that with no military certification it is neither possible to work, nor to graduate from university [...] this was the only option I had, a choice I did not want to take. However, the law requires me to perform military service, regardless of what I think, believe or what I want to do with my life [...]. However, I continue to be a conscientious objector who wants to build a nonviolent culture in his country as a strategy for reducing the context of militarization that we live in Colombia" (Peña in Decision C-728/09: 67-68). Translation by the author.

> *Hoy día, no sé qué haya pasado con ese joven que disparó inicialmente, tampoco sé que haya ocurrido con el soldado que hizo unos malintencionados cortes en las piernas de mi padre sin tratar la hemorragia; tampoco sé que haya pasado con el soldado que entorpecía la comunicación con los refuerzos sanitarios del ejército, tampoco sé qué pasó con los mandos de ese fallido operativo. Lo que sí sé es que esta experiencia me atravesó el cuerpo y la mirada dirigida al mundo. [...] Me surgió entonces la necesidad de no hacer parte de ese círculo, no colaborar con la legitimidad de la muerte en defensa por la vida.*[60] [...] (Ovalle in Decision C-728/09: 71-73)

Next, Ovalle explains his discrepancy with the use of violent means in the search for security in Colombia and explains how his conscious decision to refuse performing military service affects his possibility to exercise rights such as mobility and work:

> *Llevo años viajando con la zozobra que da la incertidumbre de no tener libreta en los retenes militares que protegen las carreteras del país. [...] Al cumplir mi plan de estudio de la universidad y comenzar a buscar mi ejercicio profesional, (pero sin título), vi como mi primer empleo se vio imposibilitado, no por incompetente en el mercado de mi profesión, sino por haber decidido no pagar la compensación militar, porque no se me respeta la posibilidad de disentir del modelo de la violencia. [...]*

[60] "Paying the fee of military compensation would have meant to assume a high debt in order to pay money to an institution I do not agree with. It would have meant adding money to the hundreds of billions of pesos spent on bullets and bombs. Paying the military compensation fee means to compensate for not putting my body in the service of arbitrariness and death. Above all, paying the military compensation fee means not being able to pay my university tuition, therefore, I postponed it indefinitely aiming to start university, which I considered was more relevant for my life at the moment. My family and I suffered the consequences of the excessive counter-insurgency military operations of the Colombian army. In 2000, my father received five of the bullets that we, Colombians, have paid for for our own security. By chance, those bullets, which were destined to cut short the life of some guerrillero, wounded my father while he was driving home after work at the municipality of Albán, Cundinamarca. Some scared and armed young man who was on the Pan-American highway that night, fired a gun by mistake in defense of his own life. Maybe it happened due to his obligatory participation in war, or for a dream of service to his country, or as happens commonly: for structural lack of educational and job opportunities. Those five shots triggered a big shooting afterwards. The incident left 68 bullet holes in my father's truck, as it was revealed by the investigation conducted by the military justice system. Today, I do not know what has happened to this young man who initially shot. I do not know what happened to the soldier who made malicious cuts into my father's legs without treating the bleeding. I do not know what has happened to the soldier who hindered the communication with the army medical help. I do not know what happened to the commanders of that failed military operation. What I do know is that this experience I went through has passed through my body and my view on the world. [...] then, I came to feel the need not to be part of that circle, not to cooperate with the legitimacy of the death in defense of life" (Ovalle in Decision C-728/09: 68-70). Translation by the author.

> *Me declaro imposibilitado para hacer parte de un grupo con el cual no me identifico por tratarse de un cuerpo armado que ejerce la violencia como medio para conseguir la seguridad; estoy imposibilitado porque desde mi cuerpo de creencias, digo que la violencia genera inevitablemente más violencia. Como ciudadano reconozco la importancia de dar un aporte para la construcción de la sociedad, ya que como dice Bernardo Toro: 'el orden social en el que vivimos fue construido por personas —nuestros padres y abuelos— continúa siendo construido por nosotros mantenido por todos'.*[61] (Ovalle in Decision C-728/09: 71-73)

Lastly there is the story of Estefanía Gómez Vásquez, a young woman who describes herself as a conscientious objector after experiencing the absence of one of her cousins who was drafted. She says:

> *Ahora, siendo objetora de conciencia y siendo la encargada de realizar el acompañamiento psicosocial a los jóvenes reclutados irregularmente y en riesgo de reclutamiento, asisto a jornadas de concentración, registro y acompaño cientos de casos donde los jóvenes son reclutados sin conocer sus derechos como exentos o aplazados; por ser hijos únicos, padres de familia, desplazados, estudiantes, o tener alguna inhabilidad física, sensorial o mental de cualquier tipo, son reclutados silenciosamente y entonces viene a mi mente la imagen de todas la mujeres; madres, esposas y abuelas, que nos acompañan en estas jornadas que esperan pacientemente un día entero para regresar con ellos a sus hogares.*
>
> *[...] Tuve la oportunidad de mostrar una obra de danza en un evento que para el 2005 los objetores de conciencia organizaron, un festival por la objeción de conciencia, donde después de bailar me invitaban a dirigirme al público y tal vez justificar por qué en medio de punk, hardcore y rap, la danza contemporánea era válida como forma de resistencia a la guerra, a lo obligatorio sin espacio a cuestionamiento y allí enuncié por primera vez, sin saber muy bien a dónde me dirigía todo esto, de manera más bien visceral, que mi cuerpo era el reflejo de lo que decidía vivir, que mi cuerpo no sería objeto, ni objetivo militar, que prestar mi cuerpo para hacer daño o para ser mutilado no era una op-*

---

[61] "For the past years whenever I travel I keep feeling anxious when approaching military checkpoints that protect the country's roads, it comes from the uncertainty of having no military certification. [...] When I finished my university courses and started looking for a job (with no diploma), I realized that getting a first job was going to be impossible, not for being incompetent in the professional market but for having decided not to pay the military compensation fee, because my dissent from the model of violence was not respected by the State. [...] I declare myself unable to be part of a group I do not support because it is an armed body that uses violence as a means to achieve security. I am unable to do it because of my beliefs. I say that violence inevitably generates more violence. As a citizen I recognize the importance of contributing to building my society, because as Bernardo Toro says: "the social order in which we live was built by people, by our parents and grandparents, and it continues being built by us all and is maintained by everyone" (Ovalle in Decision C-728/09: 68-70). Translation by the author.

> *ción, que mi cuerpo sería el espacio primero de la resistencia* [...].[62] (Gómez in Decision C-728/09: 73-74)

These testimonies illustrate that some young people in Colombia understand, perform and embody practices of peace in their daily lives that correspond to energetic, postmodern and transrational peaces (Dietrich, 2008), alongside with people who abide by modern and moral peaces.

4.2 Petition of Unconstitutionality

On 3 April 2009, the Colombian Constitutional Court received a petition of unconstitutionality[63] brought by three citizens (hereinafter petitioners)[64] who commented against the validity of part of the Colombian Conscription Law (Law 48/1993) regarding its substantive content.

According to the petitioners, Law 48/1993 violated the Constitutional rights to *freedom of conscience, freedom of worship* and *equality* of conscientious objectors to the military service, as they are not exempted from the duty to take up arms. Thus, Constitutional judges were asked to declare the unconstitutionality of Law 48/1993 in its article 27:

---

[62] "I am a conscientious objector in charge of an NGO's program to provide psycho-social support to young people who are illegally drafted or are at risk of being recruited. I attend recruitment operations to accompany the processes of registration of hundreds of young people who do not know their rights. Many of them have no siblings, have children of their own, are displaced people, students, are married or have a physical or sensorial disability of some kind, and still, they are silently recruited by the army even if the law says they should be excepted. Then it comes to my mind the image of women, their mothers, their wives and the grandmothers who accompany us during these recruitment operations waiting patiently the whole day to return home with their boys.[...] During a festival for conscientious objection organized by a group of objectors in 2005, I had the opportunity to do a dance performance. After dancing I was invited to address the public and perhaps justify why through punk, hardcore and rap, contemporary dance was a valid form of resistance towards war, towards all what is imposed with no room for questioning.There, in a rather visceral way, without really knowing where I was going with all that, I expressed for the first time that my body was a reflection of what I had decided to do with my life. I expressed that my body would not be an object, it would not be a military target. I said I refused the option of using my body to do harm or to be mutilated. I expressed that my body would be the first space for resistance to war [...]" (Gómez in Decision C-728/09: 70-71). Translation by the author.

[63] Colombian Constitution, Article 241: "The Constitutional Court is to safeguard the integrity and supremacy of the Constitution according to the strict and precise terms of this article. For this purpose, it will fulfill the following functions: [...] 4. Decide on the petitions of unconstitutionality brought by citizens against the laws, both for their substantive content as well as for errors of procedure in their form" (Constitution of Colombia, 1991: Article 241).

[64] Gina Cabarcas Macía, Antonio Barreto Rozo and Daniel Bonilla Maldonado.

> *Exenciones en todo tiempo. Están exentos de prestar el servicio militar en todo tiempo y no pagan cuota de compensación militar: a) Los limitados físicos y sensoriales permanentes. b) Los indígenas que residan en su territorio y conserven su integridad cultural, social y económica.*[65] (Law 48/1993: Article 27)

The arguments offered by the petitioners concerning rights' violations are the following. Regarding *freedom of conscience*, Constitutional Article 18 says:

> *Se garantiza la libertad de conciencia. Nadie será molestado por razón de sus convicciones o creencias ni compelido a revelarlas ni obligado a actuar contra su conciencia.*[66] (Constitución Política de Colombia, 1991: Article 18)

The argument brought in the lawsuit refers to legal obligation to 'perform acts' (*obligaciones de hacer*), as in the case of serving for the military. "When the state imposes obligations of this kind, it should first establish mechanisms to protect people's conscience" (Petitioners in Decision C-728/09: 24). Petitioners argued that when a person uses their right to freedom of conscience to oppose a legal obligation to perform some act, the state not only should listen and respect, but also offer alternatives to ensure that the person can serve the community without violating his/her freedom of conscience (Petitioners in Decision C-728/09). Regarding the right to *equality*, the Colombian Constitution states:

> *Todas las personas nacen libres e iguales ante la ley, recibirán la misma protección y trato de las autoridades y gozarán de los mismos derechos, libertades y oportunidades sin ninguna discriminación por razones de sexo, raza, origen nacional o familiar, lengua, religión, opinión política o filosófica. El Estado promoverá las condiciones para que la igualdad sea real y efectiva y adoptará medidas en favor de grupos discriminados o marginados. El Estado protegerá especialmente a aquellas personas que por su condición económica, física o mental, se encuentren en circunstancia de debilidad manifiesta y sancionará los abusos o maltratos que contra ellas se cometan.*[67] (Constitución Política de Colombia, 1991: Article 13)

---

[65] Law 48/1993, Article 27: "Exemptions at all times. Are exempt from military service at all times and pay no share of military compensation: a) Those with physical and sensory permanent disabilities. b) Indigenous people residing in their territory who preserve their cultural, social and economic integrity" (Law 48/1993: Article 27). Translation by the author.

[66] Article 18: "Freedom of conscience is guaranteed. No one will be importuned on account of his/her convictions or beliefs or compelled to reveal them or obliged to act against his/her conscience" (Constitution of Colombia, 1991: Article 18).

[67] Article 13: "All individuals are born free and equal before the law and are entitled to equal protection and treatment by the authorities, and to enjoy the same rights, freedoms, and opportunities without discrimination on the basis of gender, race, national or family origin, language, religion, political opinion, or philosophy. The State will promote the conditions necessary in order that equality may be real and effective, will adopt measures in favor of

According to the petitioners (in Decision C-728/09: 6-24), when the legislative authority establishes obligations to groups of citizens whose special conditions make them radically *different* and as such require extra-ordinary protection from the state, "there is need for the inclusion of clear mechanisms for their protection and a range of alternative obligations for conscientious objectors to serve the community" (Petitioners in Decision C-728/09: 21). About the right to freedom of worship, the Colombian Constitution states:

> *Se garantiza la libertad de cultos. Toda persona tiene derecho a profesar libremente su religión y a difundirla en forma individual o colectiva. Todas las confesiones religiosas e iglesias son igualmente libres ante la ley.* (Constitución Política de Colombia, 1991: Article 19)[68]

This right is violated in the same way of the right to freedom of conscience. While the legislative authority does not accept that some legal obligations "such as military service can go against the internal forum of some people and also accept that these types of obligations need to be replaceable by alternative ones, the state will be violating rights" (Petitioners in Decision C-728/09: 24).

Furthermore, petitioners asked the judges to harmonize their jurisprudence regarding conscientious objections on a general basis given that other types of legal objections have been recognized in Colombia with the aim of protecting the right to *equality* (interpreted as a right to diverge without being discriminated against). Hence, if other types of legal objections are valid even though there is no written law regulating them, why are objections to military service denied? Petitioners claimed that there has been recognition of objections in several other cases: to make oath in the context of legal trials (Decision T-537/93), working or studying during *Sabbath* (Decision T-982/01), joining scholar activities contrary to religious beliefs (Decision T-588/98), and medical doctors' duty to practice abortions (Decision T-209/08) (Petitioners in Decision C-728/09: 6-24).

---

groups which are discriminated against or marginalized. The State will especially protect those individuals who on account of their economic, physical, or mental condition are in obviously vulnerable circumstances and will sanction any abuse or ill-treatment perpetrated against them" (Constitution of Colombia, 1991: Article 13).

68 Article 19: "Freedom of religion is guaranteed. Every individual has the right to freely profess his/her religion and to disseminate it individually or collectively. All religious faiths and churches are equally free before the law" (Constitution of Colombia, 1991: Article 19).

4.3 DECISION C-728/09: VARIATIONS ON PEACE AND RIGHTS

During the process of analysis of the Constitutional claim regarding the revision of norms on conscientious objections to military service in Colombia, the Constitutional Court received 12 documents signed by more than 400 organizations, submitted by institutions, organizations and people who wanted to take part in the discussion, namely:

(1) The Colombian Ministry of Defense, (2) School of Law of Eafit University, (3) DeJusticia, (4) the Colombian Commission of Jurists, (5) Professors Marina Gascón Abellán y Luis Fernando Prieto Sánchez, (6) Professor Manuel Alejandro Iturralde, (7) Alba Milena Romero (supported by War Resisters' International, Conscience and Peace Tax International and Quaker United Nations Office), (8) the Colombian Mennonite Church, (9) the Collective of Conscientious Objectors (*Acción Colectiva de Objetoras y Objetores de Conciencia, ACOOC*), (10) Students of anthropology at Javeriana University and a group of conscientious objectors, (11) the Centre for Human Rights and International Litigation (*Centro de Derechos Humanos y Litigio Internacional CEDHUL*), and (12) the Colombian Attorney's General Office.

Each institution expressed their perspective on the content of the right to freedom of conscience, its importance concerning peace and violence in Colombia and how it is affected by compulsory military draft. They represent plural sectors within the Colombian society and therefore have different interpretations of peace.

Following Atienza's (2006) elaboration on law as argumentation, in the law of democratic societies, what matters the most are not only courts decisions but *the reasons* —or certain types of reasons— offered in favor to make those decisions. If legal thought can generate equally plausible justifications of rights for almost any result (Kennedy, 2002), then it is vital to analyze how different perspectives on peace lead to different *types of reasons* to accept or object the duty of military service in Colombia.

The relevant reflection from peace studies to consider in the following legal analysis points at the importance of jurists' awareness regarding the multiplicity of ways in which peace can be thought and experienced, hence, that it is possible to observe how certain types of reasons offered within legal argumentation legitimate 'absolute truths' and thus domination (structural violence). Furthermore, it is also possible to creatively offer types of reasons that legitimate non-violent legal practices. In the following section, I will contrast different lines of interpretation of the right to freedom of conscience offered in decision C-728/09 with Dietrich's (2008, 2012) five families of interpretation and see if and how the interpretation of rights in this concrete case varies along with variations of the concept of peace.

4.3.1 Energetic Perspectives

The energetic perspective on peace described in subsection 1.3.3 of this book has been used by Colombian indigenous communities to claim their freedom of conscience along with their unconditional right to object to military service. Even though Law 48/1993 exempts indigenous people from this duty, it establishes two conditions for the exception, namely: (1) permanence of the indigenous in their traditional territory and (2) maintenance of their indigenous cultural, social and economic integrity.

These requisites have been interpreted by some as an annihilation of the core of the energetic indigenous identity and perspective on peace in consideration to its incompatibility with hierarchical armed institutions. Unfortunately, Colombian indigenous organizations did not take part in the 2009 court case under examination (Decision C-728/09), which might have been due to the fact that the particular situation of indigenous refusal to military service had been already discussed in a previous court case the same year (Decision T-113/09). Therefore, although the present chapter refers to the different arguments brought in decision C-728/09 regarding a right to object military service in Cololmbia, the most relevant energetic-oriented arguments are not included in this decision but were brought up in other Constitutional cases in 1994 and 2009. In order to include this important perspective in my analysis of the five variations of peace, I will use a different source in this section: decisions C-058/94 and T-113/0. For the rest of the analisys I will use only decision C-728/09.

Decision C-058/94

The first case in which energetic-oriented arguments to refuse military service were introduced took place in 1994 (Decision C-058/94), where the Constitutional Court decided on a claim brought by the former president of the National Indigenous Organization of Colombia (ONIC), Alfonso Palma Capera. Palma argued that exceptions to military service should not only cover indigenous people who keep living in their traditional territory, but also those who for any reason have moved out to live in other regions of the country.

"There are cases when indigenous people decide to move from their traditional territory to other urban or rural areas in order to carry on academic or political projects, to work for the rights of indigenous people, or just to exchange with other Colombian cultures" (Palma in Decision C-058/94: 2-3). According to Palma, many times this is the result of intensive process of acculturation by public institutions that try to 'civilize' them, doing their best to change their identities, cultures, models of social organization and own economies. Others are displaced by the armed conflict ending up living in urban areas (Palma in Decision C-058/94: 2-3). "Indigenous people are punished for having been 'civilized'; the punishment consists of being forced to join the armed forces against their beliefs" (Palma in Decision C-058/94: 2-3).

The plaintiff in this court case claimed that the indigenous identity does not disappear from the person by moving to a city; besides, the law affects indigenous people when it discriminates between those who live in ancestral territories and those who live in urban areas. The 'multiethnic and multicultural' Constitutional principles have to go beyond mere classificatory operations of the Colombian population. It is the indigenous identity that is incompatible with the philosophy of armies and it does not depend on where the indigenous person is living at the time of drafting (Decision C-058/94: 2-3). In the context of the plurality of peaces, this contradiction between indigenous conscience and armies is a reflection of the tension between energetic and modern peaces in the legal sphere.

Decision T-113/09

The second case took place in February 2009 (Decision T-113/09) when the Court decided on a Constitutional appeal brought up by Amparo Ortega viuda de Coral, an indigenous woman who used the tutelage action (*acción de tutela*) to claim the protection of the fundamental rights of her son, Servio Francisco Coral Ortega. Previously, in 2005, she had used judiciary action to claim her son's right not to be drafted due to his indigenous ethnicity. Servio Francisco was drafted by the Army anyway in January 2005 and deployed to a high-risk area of guerrilla influence in the southern part of Colombia.

In the first instance in court, the Army alleged that by the time of recruitment, Servio Francisco had neither presented formal proof of keeping his cultural, economic, and social indigenous integrity nor of his community-based life style (Colombian Army in Decision C-058/94). All he had shown was a certification of his indigenous ethnicity issued by the indigenous authority. The army alleged that the indigenous person must prove all the requirements listed in Article 27, Law 48/1993 in order to be exempted from military service, and also claimed that the mother was not legally allowed to use judiciary action in the name of her son, since he was already above the age of 18 and therefore legally capable of going to court without parental tutelage. Under these reasons the army asked the Court to dismiss the lawsuit (Colombian Army in Decision T-113/09: 3-4).

During the legal process, it was proven that the Colombian Army was conducting recruiting operatives around indigenous territory on a regular basis, without setting a respectful and clear position against such illegal entrants (Decision T-113/09: 7-8) to which indigenous organizations responded by claiming respect towards their own ancestral law[69] and energetic-oriented perspective on peace:

> *En la Constitución Política de 1991 peleamos y logramos un reconocimiento, aunque sea teórico, de parte de este derecho ancestral, del Derecho Mayor, que hoy lo defendemos y lo defenderemos hasta el final; con ello, por la defensa de nuestra identidad cultural, se ha concluido que nuestras comunidades deben estar al margen de la confrontación armada, que nuestros jóvenes no sean involucrados en un mundo diferente al nuestro y que conduce a una culturización de guerra y confrontación a sabiendas de que somos un pueblo de Paz y con nuestra propia manera de conducir la organización y la autorregulación en nuestros pueblos, sin necesidad de recurrir a la confrontación a la que se nos quiere incluir. Los Cabildos Indígenas del Pueblo Pasto no aceptamos la incorporación de nuestros jóvenes al servicio militar.*[70] (Colombian Indigenous Organization from Pasto in Decision T-113/09: 3-4)

Regarding the energetic perspective on rights, indigenous organizations referred to the sacred relation people-nature and the knowledge of spiritual forces in relation to authority-equilibrium and harmony:

> *Los sistemas jurídicos propios [de los indígenas] se caracterizan por concepciones particulares de derecho, justicia, autoridad y poder, participación y representación [...] determinadas por los principios de armonía social, espir-*

[69] I argue that the indigenous notion of ancestral law is comparable to classic Iusnaturalism (see sub-section 2.1.1), according to which there is universal shared knowledge on justice and dignity that inspires and gives validity to written rules.

[70] "In the 1991 Political Constitution we fought for and gained recognition, albeit theoretical, of part of our ancestral law. Today we stand for and will defend our cultural identity until the end. According to this identity we have concluded that our communities should be free from armed confrontation, that our young people should not be taken into a world different from ours that leads to acculturation of war and confrontation. Knowing that we are a people of peace and conduct self-regulatory organization of our people, without resorting to the confrontation in which they want to include us. The Indigenous Councils of the Pasto region do not accept the inclusion of our young people in military service" (Indigenous organizations from Pasto in Decision T-113/09: 3-4). Translation by the author.

> *itual con la naturaleza y en equilibrio de fuerzas.*[71] (Colombian Indigenous Organization from Pasto in Decision T-113/09: 14)

A group of anthropologists affiliated with the Los Andes University commented on the role of rights' variations within *pluralistic democracies* such as the one Colombia designed in its 1991 Political Constitution. They contended that, for instance, while modern cultures have individualistic interpretations of civil rights and social responsibility, indigenous and other energetic-oriented cultures have *collective interpretations*, reflecting their communitarian social structures (Los Andes University in Decision T-113/09). In this way, rights imply the responsibility and commitment of different generations that encourage collective compliance within the group. Those alternative interpretations of rights need to be respected and protected (Los Andes University in Decision T-113/09: 29).

As said by this group of academics, in the concrete case of draftee Servio Francisco Coral Ortega, when his mother used legal action in his name —even though he was already an adult— she was fulfilling the commitment of their ancestors to struggle for the boy's chance to comply with his duty to serve his community. For each member, serving the indigenous community involves being an active part of it and contributing with their particular knowledge.

By these means, each member contributes to the collective survival of the group in the long run. In this light, this mother's claim should be accepted by the judges even if the Colombian law states that adults cannot be represented by their parents in court. Such alternative interpretation of norms takes place in the spirit of recognizing the collective variation of rights within the multiethnic Colombian nation (Los Andes University in Decision T-113/09: 29). The Constitutional Court observed this argument, declared this mother's petition as a valid alternative and ordered the army to permit the indigenous man cease his military service.

The Court interpreted norms differently in favor of recognizing legal pluralism in the Colombian society. Yet, in these two constitutional cases, the Court did not accept that indigenous people who are not living in their ancestral territories and do not have a (indigenous) community-based life style are exempt from obligatory military service. That particular claim was refused

---

[71] "[Indigenous] legal systems are characterized by particular conceptions of law, justice, authority and power, participation and representation [...] determined by the principles of social harmony, spirituality with nature and a balance of forces (Colombian Indigenous Organization from Pasto in Decision T-113/09: 14). Translation by the author.

by the use of a line of argumentation that, even though moves away from the radical modern perspective by including plurality, still rejects the integration of energetic oriented elements to build up alternative interpretations of rights (Constitutional Court in Decision T-113/09; Decision C-058/94).

The Court understood that exempting indigenous people from military service aims to protect 'national cultural diversity' because "it protects the very existence of indigenous communities as such" (Constitutional Court in Decision T-113/09). I further argue that the judges did not aim to protect the conscience or worldview of the indigenous peoples in regard to their perspective of peace. According to the Court (Decision T-113/09), given the fact that the indigenous culture focuses on the 'collective' instead of the 'individual', if the army takes male members out of their community for a year, it will affect their group dynamics and put the community at risk of disappearing, and, if indigenous communities disappear, Colombian cultural richness will disappear. Following this logic, drafting indigenous people who have already left their traditional territory will not be harmful for the community; therefore, there is no need to exempt them from military service.

In this vein, the Court has not recognized an energetic-oriented interpretation of the right to freedom of conscience of indigenous people in Colombia. As explained by anthropologists from Javeriana University (in Decision T-113/09), the Court's understanding of the indigenous identity is reduced to the territorial horizon; it formulates an essentialist, static and self-contained representation of culture. Such an understanding does not manage to incorporate elements such as cultural movement and permanent exchange (Javeriana University in Decision T-113/09: 30).

Following Dietrich's (2008, 2012) five variations of the interpretation of peace, the Court's argumentation moves away from strict modern perspectives given that it accepts the valid coexistence of different cultural groups in the legal sphere. Nonetheless, it does not integrate necessary energetic elements claimed by indigenous people as the core of their rejection of military service. In this sense, anthropologists from Javeriana University commented:

> *Los grupos humanos sin duda siempre han sido más móviles que estáticos y sus identidades menos definidas que lo que la antropología clásica ha sugerido (Gupta & Ferguson, 1992). Por el contrario se piensa que los procesos de desterritorialización de las identidades en el contexto contemporáneo se da también en los marcos de la variabilidad de los pueblos que tradicionalmente se han asociado a lo indígena, [...] la Corte [puede] 'desesencializar' las identidades y flexibilizar sus matices en el contexto de una sociedad con un mayor*

> *número de diversidades manifiestas [...]. Esto lleva a considerar que la identidad no se pierde por el sólo hecho de no estar confinada a un espacio en medio de determinados lazos sociales.*[72] (Javeriana University in Decision T-113/09: 31)

This territorial, self-contained understanding of energetic cultures in the legal sphere led the Court to restrict energetic-oriented interpretations of the right to object to military service only to the case of indigenous communities who live in ancestral territories. Indigenous people living in the rest of the territory, along with many other energetic-oriented communities in Colombia such as the Afro-Colombians of the Pacific and Caribbean Coasts, do not receive legal recognition of their diverging perspective on peace and struggle to resist the armed conflict (Lozano, 2012).

4.3.2 Moral and Modern Perspectives

In contrast to the harmonious exercises of balancing opposites or poles that inspire energetic peaces, the moral perspective on peace (addressed in subchapter 1.3.3 of his book) is based on fundamental dualisms where the pole identified as negative is to be eliminated. It is the 'ideal' of a future elimination of the dark/negative pole that defines moral peaces. In this sense, Dietrich (2009: 11) points out that in contexts of moral peaces, "the anticipation of existence replaces existence itself." Moral and modern peaces are defined by the same principles of separation and belief in absolute truths; they are both abstract and impossible to locate in the here and now (Dietrich, 2009).

Moral and modern peaces need institutions to enforce authority and secure the path to peace: "Polis, Empire, State, and Church" (Dietrich 2009: 11). When analyzing moral perspectives in decision C-728/09, at first I was focusing on the arguments brought by the Mennonite Church, most likely guided by a stereotyping thought of mine, according to which religious norms are always moral, to my surprise, I found that the arguments brought

[72] "Human groups are more mobile than static and their identities less well defined than classic anthropology has suggested (Gupta & Ferguson, 1992). On the contrary, in the contemporary context it is thought that processes of deterritorialization of identities are also valid to understand the variability of the indigenous. The Court [could] 'de-essentialise' identities and make their nuances flexible in the context of a society with a higher number of diverging identities [...] This leads to the conclusion that identity is not lost just by not being confined to a space or not being in the middle of certain social ties" (Javeriana University in Decision T-113/09: 31). Translation by the author.

by the Mennonite community were postmodern-oriented.[73] In this sense, Dietrich (2009: 11) points out that "not all norms are moral." The breaking point between energetic and moral variations on peace is when norms start being *de-contextualized* from their energetic frame and become independent, in other words, they start justifying themselves, hence turning absolute (Dietrich 2009).

Such transitions from energetic to moral worldviews "can happen during moments of social crisis, through emergency measures that become perpetual, and thus legitimate institutions and domination" (Dietrich 2009: 11). Moral and modern peaces share foundations and Dietrich categorizes them separately according to the prevalent source of authority inspiring them: god or reason. Either one turns them into absolute truths.

The Mennonite Church argued *freedom of worship* and claimed *respect* towards the "spiritual vocation leading many Mennonite Christians not to take up arms as means to peace" (Colombian Menonnite Church in Decision C-728/09: 66). They argued non-violence based on religious beliefs as the source of their conscientious objection to military service. However, despite using the religious-monotheist element in their argumentation, they explained their identification with non-violence without claiming the need to force other people in Colombia to act alike. Neither did they claim their worldview to be an absolute truth, nor did they argue against the military institution as a whole, but merely explained how the Mennonite community identifies with non-violence as a matter of principles and thus objects to military service. This is why my reading of their claim is that it is not focused on a need to eliminate other perspectives, but on the defense of the own one as a possibility to coexist in plurality.

In the constitutional revision of objectors to military service in Colombia (Decision C-728/09), moral arguments were introduced to support compulsory military service as an expression of national solidarity. When concrete reasons of conscience cannot be an exception to the legal duty to take up arms, the norm starts justifying itself; it becomes absolute and legitimates absolute truths and domination (Dietrich, 2009). When rights (such as freedom of conscience) are not contextualized to concrete people and concrete needs in concrete moments and places but are generalized, they also become independent from their purpose and energetic frame, they too start legitimat-

[73] The arguments brought by the Colombian Mennonite Church will be included in subchapter 4.2.4 corresponding to the postmodern perspectives brought by intervenors in Decision C-728/09.

ing domination. In the constitutional case of conscientious objections, the Colombian Ministry of Defense was the only intervenor offering a moral/modern perspective on peace when sustaining its calim to the Court.

Colombian Ministry of Defense

The Ministry of Defense asked the Constitutional Court to keep the text of Law 48/1993 and the general obligation to military service with no exception other than indigenous people (only those who live in their ancestral territories) and men with disabilities (Ministry of Defense in Decision C-728/09: 24-26).

Representatives of the Ministry claimed that it was wrongful to conduct a new examination of Law 48/1993 since the issue of exceptions to the military service had been already judged by the Constitutional Court in 1994 (Decision C-058/94). Furthermore, it was claimed by the Ministry that the current legal system did not include specific legislation on objections; therefore authorizations to citizens to object military service could not be given by the army or judges. "The duty to take up arms established in Article 216 of the Constitution is an unavoidable duty of the person" aiming for the common good (Ministry of Defense in Decision C-728/09: 26). The participation of the Ministry of Defense in this process reproduces the arguments used by the Constitutional Court in its jurisprudence from 1992 to October 2009 to deny the practicability of objections to military service in Colombia.

4.3.3 Postmodern Perspectives

Following the pillars of postmodern philosophy analyzed in chapter one, postmodern interpretations of rights would be those open to plurality, to more than one valid interpretation or form of exercising liberties. Groups that are excluded or discriminated against by modern discourses of rights find space in postmodern interpretations, such as those who have understandings of peace different from the modern. In this vein, postmodernity is closer to the idea of democracy in the sense of social participation without discrimination.

Most of the arguments brought to this court case are postmodern-oriented. The lawsuit containing the petition of unconstitutionality is in itself a reaction to the absolutist perspectives from which Colombian authorities (Government, Army and Juditiary) had understood peace, solidarity and the duty to perform military service since 1992. The lawsuit and the plurality of voices joining the talk, attempted to deconstruct some of the core (meta)narratives (Lyotard, 1984) upon which the norm of obligatory military service with no possible objection was sustained. Since the list of intervenors and arguments is long, I will group them by the type of reasons they discussed and will refer separately to the lawsuit's arguments.

The Lawsuit

The philosophical standpoint of the Constitutional claim that generated decision C-728/09 is postmodern. The argumentation brought in the lawsuit irradiates a pluralistic perspective to the right to freedom of conscience in Colombia. Petitioners explained that in the frame of a multiethnic and multicultural state, there has to be a possibility to have different coexisting understandings of what it means to have a good life, therefore the option to perform military service is as valid as the option to object to or to choose an alternative social service (Petitioners in Decision C-728/09: 6-24).

Following constitutional precedents in regard to equality, petitioners interpreted the right to *equality* essentially as a *right to be different.* "The Constitutional Court has referred to a right to difference; this right protects diverse understandings of *what it is to have a good life* as well as which actions to undertake according to those diverse understandings" (Petitioners in Decision C-728/09: 15). Petitioners did not integrate spiritual components of peace in their argumentation, yet, they made an important contribution by bringing the issue of pluralistic interpretation of rights to public discussion in the frame of a claim of unconstitutionality.

Now I will move into the examination of the reasons offered in the process of deconstruction of the main (meta)narratives supporting the idea of military service as an absolute duty.

The Narrative of the Historical Argument

The Colombian legal research institute *Centro de Estudios de Derecho, Justicia y Sociedad* (DeJusticia) referred to inadequate argumentation used by the Constitutional Court when it declared conscientious objections *not* to be a right in the Colombian legal system (Constitutional Court in Decision T-409/92). DeJusticia (in Decision C-728/09) called for the inadequate use of the historical argument used by the Court to deny objections as part of the conscription system,[74] by explaining that there is documentation of the Constitutional debates in 1991 showing that the National Constituent Assembly was concerned with respecting people's deep convictions against the use of arms and to hierarchical structures of relation, but considered objections to be a matter to be developed in laws rather than in the Constitution.

The Narrative of Objections as Not Forming Part of One's Freedom of Conscience

DeJusticia (in Decision C-728/09: 29-38) argued that the right to freedom of conscience does not need further legal development in order to be applied by judges. In other words, there is no need for explicit regulation in laws in order to respect this constitutional right. In this logic, given that objections to military service are an essential part of the mentioned right, the Army and judges should start accepting objections immediately.

The School of Law of Eafit University supported this idea and brought a new argument to the discussion: if conscientious objections were not an essential component of the right to freedom of conscience, the protection of the said right would be possible to require only from other citizens but never from the Colombian state (Eafit University in Decision C-728/09: 26-29). For its part, DeJusticia (in Decision C-728/09: 29-38) also alleged that conscientious objections to military service are an essential part of the right to freedom of conscience and should be interpreted according to the deep pluralist framework provided in articles 1, 7, 8, 13 and 16 of the Colombian Constitution. "Military service is one of the duties that potentially affect people's conscience the most since it involves the use of arms and joining a totalitarian institution, thus not including the possibility to object it as part of the right to freedom of conscience mutilates the very core of the right" (DeJusticia in Decision C-728/09: 29-38).

According to DeJusticia (in Decision C-728/09: 29-38), the collision between the right to freedom of conscience and the duty to military service should be resolved in favor of the right. "Since *freedom of conscience* is a fundamental right and the duty to serve the military institution is open to exceptions, the duty should not be an exception to the right but the other way

---

[74] The historical argument explained above in subchapter 4.1.3.

around: the right can be an exception to the duty."[75] According to DeJusticia, military service affects an objector's conscience *intensively,* while objections affect the state only slightly (DeJusticia in Decision C-728/09: 29-38).

In the same vein, law professor Manuel Alejandro Iturralde (acting here with no institutional afilliation), the Center of Human Rights and International Litigation, and the Human Rights Clinic of the Florida International University (in Decision C-728/09: 65), claimed the essential role of legal objections within the right to freedom of conscience by referring to examples of foreign legislations such as the Brazilian, Paraguayan, Australian, and South African, which all recognize objections to military service even though they all have different cultures and legal systems. "All these States have incorporated a progressive and growing view towards conscientious objectors that the Colombian Constitutional Court should emulate" (Iturralde and others in Decision C-728/09: 65). The same argument was brought by the Center of Human Rights and International Litigation (CEDHUL) (in Decision C-728/09: 77). The Colombian Mennonite Church also argued that there are Christian expressions and traditions in Colombia whose basis is nonviolence, including refusal to the use of arms and, therefore, forcing a person to join an armed institution is contravening his/her freedom of worship and conscience.

Concerning freedom of conscience, the UN has consistently referred to objections to military service as essential part of its exercise (Colombian Commision of Jurists –CCJ– in Decision C-728/09: 52). For instance in 1978 the UN recognized the right to object to military or police service used to enforce apartheid (Resolution 33/165, 1978), in 1989 it emphasized that states should introduce alternative ways of social service that are compatible to objectors' concerns and do not punish objectors with jail (*Resolution 1987/46*, 1989). In 1998, the UN called on states to change legislation and practices that contribute to the discrimination of objectors to military service (Resolution 1998/77)[76] (CCJ in Decision C-728/09: 52).

Moreover, in 2004, the UN referred to the particular case of Colombia expressing preoccupation about the exercise of the right to freedom of conscience given that the Colombian legislation did not allow objections to mili-

---

[75] DeJusticia takes this argument from the dissenting votes of Judges Cifuentes, Gaviria and Martínez in Decision C-511/94, when the Constitutional Court reasserted the inexistence of a right to object to military service in Colombia.

[76] For a comprehensive account on UN decitions on conscientious objections to military service from 1970 to date, see Takemura (2009: 19-81).

tary service. On this occasion, the UN recommended the allowance of alternative societal services other than the military, with no punishing effects (UN Human Rights Committee, 2004) (CCJ in Decision C-728/09).

The Narrative of Obligatory Military Service as Indispensable for National Peace

The School of Law of Eafit University disputed that the general obligation for all Colombian men to take up arms might be a *suitable* measure aimed to a legitimate purpose, such as defending national independence and public institutions, but certainly it was not a *necessary* measure (Eafit University in Decision C-728/09). The ultimate aim of the duty to take up arms is *national peace* and peace is possible not only via armies, but by many other ways of social contribution that do not necessarily consist of joining an armed institution (Eafit University in Decision C-728/09).

The opening of the legal system to conscientious objections neither means that the national army will disappear altogether nor that it will make peace inaccessible (Eafit University in Decision C-728/09: 26-29). According to this group, the possibility to object to military service along with the creation of alternative social services is an option to harmonize two conflicting legal norms: (1) the general duty to contribute to national peace and defend the Constitutional order with (2) the right to freedom of conscience of all people (Eafit University in Decision C-728/09: 26-29).

The thought of military service as an *unnecessary* measure to preserve national unity (Eafit University in Decision C-728/09: 26-29), was used by the UN Human Rights Committee in the case *Yeo-Bum Yoon and Myung-Jing Choi vs. Republic of Korea* (UN Human Rights Committee, 2007). In this case, the Korean state alleged that its refusal to accept objections to military service was a *necessary* measure to keep the public capability to defend the nation and maintain social unity.

The UN Human Rights Committee (2007) alleged that an increasing number of states who keep obligatory draft had introduced alternative social services aiming to respect objectors' right to freedom of conscience, and still were able to keep their national defense systems. The Korean state was considered not to have demonstrated what concrete disadvantage it would suffer by accepting legal objections to military service and creating alternative options of social service.

The committee decided that there was no justification from the Korean state to neglect Yeo-Bum Yoon and Myung-Jing Choi's freedom of conscience by forcing them to perform military service against their will, hence decided the case in their favor. According to several intervenors in the Colombian court case, this precedent should be respected by the Colombian Constitutional Court (Eafit University, DeJusticia, CCJ, Alba M. Romero, CEDHUL and the Colombian Attorney's General Office in Decision C-728/09).

One more important element brought to the discussion was the issue of *proportionality*. If the sacrifice of human rights is indispensable to obtain a legitimate benefit, then the legal duty is proportional. Following this argument, rejecting legal objections to military service in Colombia is a disproportionate measure to keep national peace, since peace can be approached by a variety of social services others than the armed one. Because it is not necessary, objectors' sacrifice of their right to freedom of conscience is not proportional, thus this situation places objectors in a position of disadvantage (Eafit University in Decision C-728/09: 26-29).

The CCJ —whose amicus curiae was supported by 24 other human rights organizations[77]— turned to Moskos & Chambers (1993) to explain that some countries have opted for alternative services that are closer to the idea of positive peace (Galtung, 1996). One of the cases is Germany, where draftees can alternatively work as artisans, ambulance drivers, rescuers, or social workers and serve people with reduced abilities (CCJ in Decision C-728/09: 38-63). Similar ideas were presented by the Colombian Mennonite Church (in Decision C-728/09: 66) and Alba Milena Romero (supported by War Resisters International, Conscience and Peace Tax International and Quaker United Nations Office) (in Decision C-728/09: 66-67).

---

[77] Comisión Internacional de Juristas, Asociación por los Derechos Civiles (ADC), El Centro de Derechos Humanos Miguel Agustín Pro Juárez, American Friends Service Committee (AFSC), Servicio Paz y Justicia del Ecuador (Serpaj-Ecuador), grupo venezolano de Red de Apoyo por la Justicia y la Paz, Personería de Medellín, Escuela de Derecho y Ciencia Política de la Universidad Industrial de Santander, Semillero de Jóvenes Investigadores en Jurisprudencia y Activismo Constitucional adscrito a la Universidad de Santander UDES, Fundación Menonita Colombiana para el Desarrollo (MENCOLDES), Centro de Investigación y Educación Popular (CINEP), Equipo de Coordinación Nacional del Proceso de Comunidades Negras en Colombia (PCN), organización Colombia Diversa, Red Nacional de Mujeres, Corporación Humanas –Centro Regional de Derechos Humanos y Justicia de Género, Organización Corporación Mujeres Católicas por el Derecho a Decidir, Corporación Sisma Mujer, organización Humanidad Vigente, Corporación AVRE, Corporación Compromiso, Asociación Líderes en Acción, Corporación de Apoyo a Comunidades Populares (CODACOP), and Asamblea Permanente de la Sociedad Civil por la Paz (Decision C-728/09: 58-60).

Peter Wood Stucky, the representative leader of the Mennonite Church in Colombia along with 342 more people[78] pointed out that there is a long historic line of rejection of all forms of armed expression from religious perspectives in Colombia, which the legislation has not recognized as valid. "It is the understanding of the Mennonite Church that rather than weakening public institutions, objections to military service will strengthen ethical pillars that are essential for peace and common good" (Colombian Mennonite Church in Decision C-728/09: 66).

The Narrative of National Duties as Prevailing over Rights

Colombian professor of law Diana Durán Smela joined the discussion to support the petitioners' claims by bringing the concept of balancing (*ponderación*) rights and duties (Durán in Decision C-728/09: 63-65). Following Gascón and Prieto, Durán Smela proposed that balancing rights and duties is an exercise that judges make in every particular case aimed at finding a solution that is respectful of both. Balancing exercises are an argumentative task, so they use argumentation to escape tyranny (Durán in Decision C-728/09: 63-65).

By the use of argumentation, judges transform Constitutional guarantees and principles into concrete rights. In this vein, the right to freedom of conscience in Colombia should be respected, also in the case of disagreement with the use of arms for purposes of national defense, with no need for further legislation regulating objections, the mere existence of the right to freedom of conscience is enough to make valid objections (Durán in Decision C-728/09: 63-65). Durán also discussed that there is already a legal instrument to defend human rights in Colombia called 'tutelage action' (*acción de tutela*) that should serve objectors when there is conflict between the persons' conscience and any legal duty.[79]

One more voice pointing at the situation of domination under which objectors find themselves in Colombia was that of the Colombian Attorney General's Office.[80] This institution sustained that "conscientious objectors

---

[78] Names were not transcribed in decision C-728/09, but available in pages 285 to 306 of the original case file.

[79] This intervention was supported by Guillermo Escobar Roca, leader professor of Constitutional Law at the University of Alcalá in Madrid along with the Spanish Association for International Human Rights Law (in Decision C-728/09:63-65).

[80] The Attorney General's Office (Procuraduría General de la Nación) is a public institution overseeing the public conduct of those in authority. It is not a judicial institution but one of

should be exempt from military service in Colombia and their obligation compensated with alternative services" (Colombian Attorney General's Office in Decision C-728/09: 77). According to the Attorney General's Office, forcing people to perform military service against their ethical convictions contravenes the very principle of human dignity and the right to freedom of conscience. Therefore, in the search for peaceful and democratic relations, the national legislation needs to identify alternative services for objectors according to the standards of international law (Resolution 1998/77); namely, services of civil, not combative character that serve society and are not punitive.

4.3.4 Transrational Perspectives

As addressed in chapter one of this book, Dietrich's (2008) findings in peace research provoke the realization that we need to surrender to the *insufficiency* of mere rational means to deal with peace and conflict matters. With the term *transrational peaces* Dietrich proposes an approach to peace that reintegrates the energetic human component in the field of peace and conflict studies. His proposal is that, through this reintegration, human emotional capabilities could be used to perform non-violent practices and connect with others in compassionate and respectful ways. Transrational peaces come out of twisting the postmodern, modern, moral and energetic perspectives to peace, taking the best of each and learning from their limitations.

In this light, if legal practice is to be used to facilitate concrete situations of positive peace, then transrational interpretations of rights need to twist different approaches to peace. They need to include the rational legal analysis by taking pluralism (non-discrimination) from the postmodern, a sense of order and structure from the modern, a sacred sense of human life/dignity from the moral, and lastly, from the energetic, the essential role of human emotional capabilities to harmonize opposites: creativity, care, love, compassion, empathy and capacity for transformation. Not embracing these capabilities is what brings limitations to merely rational approaches to peace.

---

control. The Attorney General is also charged with safeguarding human rights and intervening in litigations in the name of the people in the defense of the public interest (Procuraduría General de la Nación, República de Colombia, 2011).

The following intervenors used peace in the plural while analyzing the case of objections to military service. Moreover, they overcame the limits of cultural categorization established by the Constitutional Court in its former jurisprudence (Decisions T-113/09; T-409/92) when it assumed that only indigenous people who live in ancestral territories would have their own perspective on peace clashing with military institutions. They asked for the recognition of the energetic component in all people.

Colombian Collective of Conscientious Objectors (ACOOC)

I have presented the reasons offered by this Association earlier (subchapter 4.1.5) when I referred to dissenting voices claiming the need for a more pluralistic interpretation of the right to freedom of conscience in Colombia, specifically concerning military service. Hence, in this section I will mention it very briefly, only to point out at its transrational approach.

Like the group of anthropology students from Javeriana University, the Collective of Conscientious Objectors (in Decision C-728/09: 66-69) also twisted energetic and rational elements to build up their argumentation. Besides suggesting a different logic from which to interpret the rights' discourse in the frame of the nation-state, this group also resorted to the notion of embodied peaces, nonviolent practices in the here and now and to the decision to deal with conflictive opposites in inclusive rather than exclusive ways.

"Military service is a violation of the intimate convictions on non-violence in which we base our practices" (ACOOC in Decision C-728/09: 67). They further asserted that "[w]e defend an attitude of respect for otherness and care for the other, of expressing sensitivity; we defend horizontal models of relation, solidarity, listening and non-violent solution of conflicts; all these elements make it irreconcilable for us to join a military institution" (ACOOC in Decision C-728, 2009: 67).

This group said they are convinced of the need to express solidarity by working for their country from a standpoint other than the armed one: "this is the way we have decided to face the reality of our country still at war after six decades of armed confrontation, the use of arms has aimed to achieve peace but has brought no sustainable solution" (ACOOC in Decision C-728/09: 67).

Students of Anthropology from Javeriana University and a Group of Conscientious Objectors[81]

Some students of anthropology from the Javeriana University in Bogotá, along with a group of conscientious objectors, combined energetic and rational elements to put together their claim for the respect of freedom of conscience regarding military service. They argued that many people's lives are negatively affected by the "old practice" of compulsory drafting and mentioned the need for change in this regard (Anthropology students and objectors in Decision C-728/09: 69-77).

"While the Colombian society is facing an armed conflict, those citizens that refuse the use of arms for reasons of conscience are punished by the state, which forces young men to arm themselves and take part in the war" (Anthropology students and objectors in Decision C-728/09: 69). These intervenors pointed out that there is higher investment in public policies of security than in policies of education in Colombia. Those who refuse military service face two possibilities: "paying the fee of military compensation (only available to do those with privileged social positions and who support funding armed institutions) or not buying it and consequently losing the chance to work, study and move freely around the country" (Anthropology students and objectors in Decision C-728/09).

In the context of the plurality of peaces, this statement shows that the Colombian state's policy on security uses legal institutions to construct the *modern* approach to peace as a legal obligation. Consequently, it punishes other approaches to peace. This practice is the result of an absolute denial of the energetic human component and fuels separation considering the important role of energetic traditions within the multicultural and multiethnic composition of the Colombian society.

In fact, more energetic-oriented Colombian communities, such as indigenous and Afro-Colombians, struggle to resist armed conflict by restoring to art and creative practices.[82] Moreover, sectors of the urban population who have energetic-oriented perspectives on peace practice active non-violence with great effort,[83] as is the case of conscientious objectors to military service. This is how many people in Colombia find themselves in a legal limbo,

---

[81] See their names in subsection 4.1.4.

[82] For instance by performing traditional music, for detailed analysis on how Afro-Colombians of the South Pacific Coast resist armed practices by performing music see Lozano (2012).

[83] For further information on communities performing active non-violence (in the here and now) to resist armed conflict in Colombia, see Echavarría (2010: 177-218).

because homogenizing peace policies focused on security oblige them to practice perspectives of peace *different from their own* (Dietrich & Sützl, 2006).

The group of anthropology students and objectors used testimonies to explain how objectors' inner peace, family dynamics and social environment are perturbed by obligatory conscription. Those testimonies are the clearest *contextualization* offered for the rights discussion in decision C-728/09. In those testimonies, there are elements that besides approaching the rational rights discourse also refer to human emotions, vulnerability, search for harmony and intention to deal with opposites in non-violent ways. They talked about peace not as a consequence in the future, but as experienced in the here and now, for example, by the possibility to exercise their freedom of conscience in the frame of military service.

These intervenors (Anthropology students and objectors in Decision C-728/09) talked about non-violent practices, embodied peaces and included aspects that are hardly ever considered in merely rational discussions on military service, such as the consequences for women and community as a whole. As mentioned before, a young objector woman said, "It comes to my mind the image of women, draftee's mothers, wives and grandmothers who accompany us during these recruitment operations waiting patiently for a whole day to return home with their boys" (Gómez in Decision C-728/09: 73).

The Constitutional Court (in Decision T-113/09) mentioned the need to protect indigenous people from forced drafting, since their sense of community is very strong, hence their community dynamics are disturbed when a male member is taken away for one year (Constitutional Court in Decision T-113/09). I argue that certainly many other communities in Colombia have strong community bonds that are also perturbed when one of its male members is taken away for a year of forced military service. Many other communities (families, groups of friends, organizations, neighbors) are disturbed when a member is drafted against his will. In this sense, what the transrational perspective offers is precisely the possibility to recognize and include energetic elements of 'modern' societies and used them along with the achievements of modernity for more integral approaches to peace.

Regarding embodied peaces, the testimony of Estefanía Gómez reaffirms the practices of positive peace within one's own body: "contemporary dance is a valid form of resistance towards war, towards all what is imposed with no room for questioning" (Gómez in Decision C-728/09: 74). Gómez explains that she first expressed her decision to become an objector to military service by dancing: "In a rather visceral way, I expressed for the first time that my body was a reflection of what I had decided to do with my life (...) that my body would not be an object, it would not be a military target" (Gómez in Decision C-728/09: 74) in a way that does not exactly follow the legal rules of conscription in Colombia but does indeed refer to positive peace (Galtung, 1996). Gómez said, "I refused the option of using my body to do harm or to be mutilated. I expressed that my body would be the first space for resistance to war" (Gómez in Decision C-728/09: 74).

4.3.5 Change of Judicial Precedent

As a consequence of this petition of unconstitutionality and following discussion, the Colombian Constitutional Court changed its own precedent on conscientious objections to military service held since 1992. In decision C-728/09[84] the Court recognized such objections to be an essential component of the right to freedom of conscience, and exhorted the Congress to regulate its practice along with alternative (civil) forms of social service (Constitutional Court in Decision C-728/09: 80-117).

From October 2009 onwards, conscientious objectors at risk of forced drafting can ask for the protection of their right to freedom of conscience by the use of the tutelage action (*acción de tutela*).

Case Decision

In its decision the Court was to decide if article 27 of Law 48/1993 —that establishes exemptions from military service at all times— should be declared unconstitutional because it omitted conscientious objectors, and such omission was contrary to objectors' right to freedom of conscience (Article 18 Colombian Constitution).

Even though the Court decided in favor of objections, it did not declare the unconstitutionality of article 27, considering that it did not 'omit' conscientious objectors. According to the Court, the case of conscientious objectors was not comparable to the other two cases listed in the mentioned norm, namely: (1) men with physical and sensorial disabilities, and (2) members of indigenous communities who live in their ancestral territories and keep indigenous social, cultural and economic integrity.

[84] The decision was issued in October 2009 and a summary of the decision was published by the court, but the full text of the decision including the dissenting votes was published only on 30 August 2010 (Decision C-728/09: 120).

For the Court, while article 27 refers to some 'objective' conditions for people to be exempted from military service, objections refer to 'subjective' conditions; those two different situations did not have to be dealt with in the same norm (Constitutional Court in Decision C-728/09: 80-117). In this order, the Court said that the omission was not to be found in article 27 (Law 48/1993) but in the Colombian legal system as a whole.

However, in contrast to their former jurisprudence, this time the judges have interpreted human rights' norms in a different way, concluding that objections to military service are an essential part of the fundamental right to freedom of conscience and as such, they should be respected. This approach means a new legal line of argumentation in Colombia regarding the legitimation of alternative practices of solidarity and a right to think and experience peace in plural ways.

New Types of Reasons

Since legal theory considers peace as the ultimate aim of law, and considering that what is significant in this study about plural peaces are not the legal decisions but the *types of reasons* offered in favor of those decisions (Atienza, 1999), I want to examine how the Constitutional Court moved from the idea of 'national' solidarity and sovereignty as absolute truths, to accepting objections to military service and alternative forms of solidarity.

"The Constitutional Court finds that there are several reasons to move aside from its *former jurisprudence* on objections to military service" (Constitutional Court in Decision C-728/09: 109): first, because a harmonizing reading of the rights to freedom of conscience and worship, along with norms of international Human Rights Law, shows that objections are, indeed, a fundamental right (Constitutional Court in Decision C-728/09: 109). If freedom of conscience is "not being forced to act against one's own conscience," then who is forced to perform military service while dissenting from armed institutions will certainly suffer right's violation (Constitutional Court in Decision C-728/09: 109).

Regarding the *historical argument*, "the Court steps away from its former understanding according to which the National Constituent Assembly had rejected the idea of including the right to object to military service expressly in the Constitution and thus such right did not exist in Colombia" (Constitutional Court in *Decision C-728/09*: 109). Now the Court understands that this reading does not correspond to the guarantee of "not being forced to act against the own conscience." Given that freedom of conscience has been considered by the National Constituent Assembly as a fundamental right to be protected, there is no need for further formal regulation in order to guarantee its exercise (Constitutional Court in Decision C-728/09: 109-110).

Based on international human rights' norms and jurisprudence, the Court has recognized other types of legal objections in Colombia, related for instance to labor, education and profession. In this opportunity, the Court wants to harmonize its jurisprudence and respond to the observation made in 2004 by the United Nations Human Rights Committee concerning the exercise of freedom of conscience in Colombia (UN Human Rights Committee, 2004) recommending the allowance of alternative services other than the military, with no punishing effects (Constitutional Court in Decision C-728/09: 111).

Concerning the principle of *'solidarity'* and its close connection to forced military service, "the Court considers that it is not reasonable to oblige a person to perform military service when the aim of such obligation is to contribute to the nation's protection and to facilitate social cohesion" (Constitutional Court in Decision C-728/09: 110), because such unity can be achieved by other means as well. It does not have to be only via military service, which in the case of conscientious objectors implies a deep contradiction between the legal duty and one's own ethics (Constitutional Court in Decision C-728/09: 110).

With this argumentation and following Dietrich's (2008) five variations on peace presented in chapter one, I argue that the Constitutional Court moved from a *modern-oriented concept of peace*, one that legitimized an 'absolute' understanding of solidarity and freedom of conscience, towards a *postmodern perspective of peace*, that leads to the legitimation of a plurality of equally valid truths expressed in non-discrimination and the right to perform different peace practices.

Dissenting Votes

The Constitutional Court is composed of nine judges. In this case, the nine judges unanimously agreed upon the idea that objections to military service are essential part of the right to freedom of conscience and as such should be protected in Colombia. Of the nine judges, four[85] dissented partially from the case ruling (Decision C-728/09) because of the following reasons.

[85] María Victoria Calle Correa, Juan Carlos Henao Pérez, Jorge Iván Palacio Palacio and Luis Ernesto Vargas Silva.

Contrary to what was stated in the decision, the understanding of the dissenting judges is that article 27 (Law 48/1993) did omit objectors to military service. This implies that there is no such a thing as 'objective' conditions in the case of indigenous people to be exempted from military service. The exceptions in article 27 aim to protect people who otherwise would have to carry a 'disproportionate share' by performing military service (Dissenting votes in Decision C-728/09: 123-124).

Following the dissenting voices, indigenous people are not exempted because of an 'objective' condition, the exception should be understood as aiming to protect their special worldview, spiritual practices, and sense of community, "which places them in the way of non-violence and the systematic rejection of all forms of violence, especially if it is organized, collective, formalized and institutionalized" (Dissenting votes in Decision C-728/09: 124). Therefore, regarding military service, the case of conscientious objectors is comparable, although not identical, to the case of indigenous people. They both aim to protect freedom of conscience and the right of being different (non-discrimination) (Dissenting votes in Decision C-728/09: 124).

The group of judges with dissenting votes focused the analysis more on the actual possibility for different people to be able to exercise freedom of conscience than on the strict categorization of exceptions to military service. In their arguments, they attend to the inner element or intention to perform non-violence that *any* person can have, regardless of his/her affiliation to a group or community. They understood that non-indigenous people can also express elements of energetic peace the same way as members of indigenous communities can voluntarily join the army (Dissenting votes in Decision C-728/09) and the state should not perturb those conscious decisions but create conditions for respectful coexistence in plurality. This step towards more integral approaches to peace in the argumentation of rights seems to start overcoming the strict separation of cultural categories according to which the former jurisprudence in 1992 (Decision T-409/92) had ruled the right to freedom of conscience in the frame of military service.

Unfortunately, these votes were minority within the Constitutional Court in decision C-728/09 and more 'linguistic exchange' (Atienza, 1999) will need to take place before the idea of transrational peace becomes more accepted for argumentation of rights in Colombia. In the meantime, the new possibility to claim postmodern and energetic-oriented perspectives on peace in the frame of forced military service is a motive to celebrate. The beauty of this constitutional process from the eyes of a peace researcher is the possibility to analyze the relation between the myriad interpretations brought to it and conclude that peace, indeed, can be thought differently.

As shown in this case study, different understandings of peace lead to a multiplicity of ways in which rights can be argued in concrete situations and in which concepts of one/national peace and culturally diverse peaces are used in legal argumentation. In the following table, in order to illustrate my point, I summarize the arguments presented in the constitutional case of conscientious objections to military service in Colombia, by grouping them according to Dietrich's (2008) five variations on peace.

Table 1. Arguments in Decision C-728/09 in relation to Dietrich's (2008, 2012) families of interpretation of Peace

Intervenor	Energetic	Moral / Modern
	• Indigenous organizations (In Decisions C-058/94 and T-113/09)	• Colombian Ministry Of Defense • Constitutional Court (In Decision T-409/92)
	Postmodern	**Trans-rational**
	• Plaintiffs • Eafit University School of Law • Colombian Commission of Jurists (CCJ) • UN Human Rights Committee (quoted by plaintiffs and others) • DeJusticia • Various professors of Law • Alba M. Romero, supported by War Resisters' International, Conscience and Peace Tax International and Quaker United Nations Office • Colombian Mennonite Church • Centre for Human Rights and International Litigation (CEDHUL) • Attorney's General Office of Colombia • Constitutional Court (In Decision C-728/09)	• Students of Anthropology Javeriana University and group of objectors • Colombian Collective of Conscientious Objectors (ACOOC) • Dissenting Judges • School of Anthropology Andes University (In Decision T-113/09)

*All arguments are cited in sentence C-728/09 unless otherwise indicated.

Author: Catalina Vallejo

CONCLUSION

Taking up arms in the name of peace is a reflection of the modern approach to peace. The same corresponds to the *national* way of expressing solidarity. In this vein, arguing on a right to understand and express peace in ways that diverge from the modern is bringing the plurality of peaces into legal action.

Conscientious objections are a particular form of civil disobedience. The Colombian conscription system established in Law 48/1993 does not include an exemption from military service for conscientious objectors but conceived exceptions only for indigenous men and men with physical or mental disabilities. This fact was interpreted as a violation of the right to freedom of conscience of draftees whose perspectives on peace diverge from the modern. The law establishes strict penalty against draftees who do not comply with the military duty, basically to the extent of inflicting their civil death.

In decision C-728/09 of the Colombian Constitutional Court there is a summary of the constitutional discussion that took place after a group of jurists brought a claim asking the Court to declare the unconstitutionality of part of the conscription law. Their argument was that by not allowing objections to military service, the conscription law violates the right to freedom of conscience of draftees who do not agree with the modern peace based on security.

Such claim provoked the participation of more than 400 organizations from a plurality of sectors in the Colombian society, they all presented different perspectives on the right to object to military service and dissented from the militarization effort of the Colombian government as a means to peace. Those arguments on rights reflect Dietrich's (2008) variations on peace: the energetic, the modern, the postmodern and the transrational peaces.

The Constitutional Court's previous jurisprudence on this particular topic (Decision T-409/92) denied the possibility to object to military service for reasons of conscience by arguing that the military duty was an expression of national solidarity necessary for the achievement of a common good. Consequently, the sacrifice of individual interests was justified in the name of the general interest of the Colombian nation.

The result of the constitutional claim brought in 2009 was a change in the jurisprudence regarding objections to military service. From October 2009 onwards, draftees can use legal objections to validly refuse military service.

If the army rejects objection claims, objectors can use legal action to exercise their right to freedom of conscience.

The Court accepted arguments associated to cultural variations on peace, according to which understandings of peace beyond the borders of the *sovereign nation* are also valid in legal argumentation. It is the freedom of conscience that guarantees the expression of diverging perspectives on peace.

Concluding Remarks

I started this work by pointing at the shocking evidence on the escalation of violence at the grassroots' level in Colombia since 2004 (CNP, 2010; INMLCF, 2009; Semana, 2009; 2011a). Paradoxically, this phenomenon is taking place after the institutionalization of a security policy (Presidencia de la República y Ministerio de Defensa de Colombia, 2003) strategically designed by the government in 2002 to achieve a system of one/national peace.

This particular conceptualization of peace has led to the discursive construction of the identity of an 'enemy' amongst nationals. Such an 'enemy', whoever he or she may be, is to be excluded from the nation in the name of peace. In order to exclude the 'evil' amongst us, the government has adopted a policy of militarization. Consequently, the national army is conducting military operations across the country with the order to execute as many members of non-state armed groups as possible. Statistics of dead people in combat are proudly shown by the government and the army as positive results in the fight for peace (Ministerio de Defensa Nacional - República de Colombia, 2010; El Espectador, 2010; Semana, 2010).

In this context, following and supporting the model of one/national peace based on security has become a legal duty for Colombians, in particular for young men who must perform military service. They are the ones most clearly in charge of the physical extermination of the 'enemy'. This situation has led to a growing interest in legal objections to military service for reasons of conscience, which until 2009 where forbidden by the law. In this way, the one/national peace constitutes a legal obligation and consequently excludes the expression of different perspectives on peace.

Until 2009, the Colombian Constitutional Court had interpreted the right to object to military service (part of the right to freedom of conscience) from the lenses of the one/national conceptualization of peace (Decision T-409/92, 1992). As a result, the duty to comply with the military service was exclusively understood as an expression of solidarity with focus on the sovereignty of the nation-state. According to this interpretation, the borders of the nation-state set the limits where solidarity and peace can take place.

In October 2009, the Colombian Constitutional Court issued decision C-728/09 in response to a claim for the recognition of conscientious objections to military service. That claim was supported and signed by more than 400 organizations from different associations, bringing a plurality of arguments regarding the need for legal protection of diverging perspectives on peace.

As a result of this legal process, the Court changed its own precedent and recognized that objecting to the use of arms as a means to peace is an essential part of the right to freedom of conscience.

Beyond one/national peace there is a plurality of peaces

Having set this situation as my research problem, at the early beginnings of my investigation for this book, I posed a query pointing at the conceptualization of peace behind the interpretation of rights: *In the case of conscientious objection to military service in Colombia, how does the legal argumentation of the right to freedom of conscience vary according to the five cultural variations of peace, i.e. energetic, moral, modern, postmodern and transrational peaces?*

To answer my research question, I proposed an interdisciplinary methodology, connecting the field of legal studies with contemporary peace research and choosing the jurisprudence on objections to military service in Colombia as the particular case in which to focus the analysis.

In chapter one, I examined the philosophy of the *plurality of peaces* proposed by Dietrich (2008), which is the peace perspective encouraged by the UNESCO Manifesto 2000. From a postmodern perspective, Dietrich (2006a, 2008) criticizes the radicalization of rational conceptualizations of peace that follow the model of *one/absolute* truth and therefore justify the use of violence against diverging groups as means to achieve the one/national peace.

The one/national peace is, in fact, only one of the many cultural variations of peace. Dietrich categorizes it as an 'absolute' understanding of peace (moral/modern peaces) and enlists it along with other cultural variations, i.e. energetic, postmodern and transrational peaces (Dietrich, 2008). After presenting a postmodern critic to the conceptualization of the 'one-world' peace, Dietrich suggests surrendering to the insufficiency of mere rational means to understand peace and conflict and proposes a re-integration of the spiritual human component present in the energetic perspective. Such reinterpretation is known as the *transrational* approach to peace. It is a frame in which peace is understood more as an attitude and human capability than a status, and alternative practices of solidarity are considered of high value. This is the framework I used for the subsequent study of the conscription law and situation of increasing use of violence in Colombia.

Relation between legal studies and peace research

In chapter two, I moved toward the study of the role of peace in the legal theory and practice, and the model of peace used by the law. I found that there is abundant literature supporting the idea that law and social dynamics inform each other. National law lays on the existence of the Hobbesian nation-state, which is built upon the precepts of the absolute power of a strong state. Following Dietrich's (2008) variations on peace, within the national frame, law is based on a fundamental separation of correct/legal and incorrect/illegal, hence it can foster cultural violence. Nonetheless, law is understood to exist in more contexts than the national, for instance, native communities use coactive norms as a tool for organization, which means that the law is not a petrified institution but open for transformation according to cultural transformations or variations.

By reading legal literature it became clear that the law is traversed by the concept of peace. Legal institutions are born out of the search for ordered and harmonious social relations and all acts of legal interpretation are shaped by an underlying ideal of peace. Given the essential role of peace for the law and following Atienza's (1999) idea on law as a never-ending process of argumentation and linguistic exchange, I came to the conclusion that cultural variations of peace have an effect on the way rights are argued and used.

Beyond universal rights there are plural interpretations

In chapter three, I narrowed down the general legal analysis to Human Rights Law, which is the relevant set of norms used in the case of objections to military service in Colombia. I found that all human rights' norms are founded upon the concept of human dignity, which means that the suffering of all human beings matters equally, with no discrimination whatsoever. However, when the concept of human dignity is used within the frame of national legal systems, the rights' discourse is influenced by rational narratives that *justify* exclusions: discrimination becomes legal. This is the case of the peace strategy based on security that has been taking place in Colombia since 2002. Dynamics of pseudo-speciation and dehumanization try to exclude people over their identification with certain groups.

The model of national peace based on security designed in the Colombian security policy justifies that people with 'deviated' political identities (Echavarría, 2010) *deserve* to lose their human dignity; therefore, by evoking a perfect prospect of common good to be achieved in the future (Muñoz, 2006) their human rights do not have to be respected any more (Arendt, 1966). Practices of solidarity become violent and limited to the borders of the nation-state (Hardt & Negri, 2009). The critique of the universality of human rights from the perspective of the *Transrational Peaces* focuses on the homogenization of human needs.

Under the understanding that the respect of rights is relevant for concrete situations of peace, then it becomes necessary to interpret and use rights in the same way as peace is understood: as relative, contextual, and relational.

Freedom of conscience as a right to plural peaces

In chapter four, I studied the argumentation of the right to freedom of conscience in Colombia, concretely regarding its use to object military service, and came to the conclusion that legal argumentation varies according to different perspectives on peace. What is unavoidable are the power relations amongst the peaces within legal contexts, since the interpretation assumed by the authority, in this case the Constitutional Court, is to be the dominant perspective after its new jurisprudence is published. This is how even when cultural variations on peace penetrate the rights' discourse and even manage to transform it every now and then, still the law is a modern institution based on hierarchical power structures and coactive practices.

In decision C-728/09, intervenors expressing *energetic-oriented* perspectives on peace (see Table 1, subchapter 4.3.5) rejected the use of violence by principle and refused the idea of constructing the identity of 'enemy' as means to peace (ACOOC, Students of anthropology and objectors in Decision C-728/09; Indigenous organizations and School of Anthropology Andes University in Decision T-113/09). Since the energetic perspective perceives peace as harmony out of opposites, the mere idea of eliminating the opposite pole contradicts the very ontology of the perspective. They also called the judges' attention to the fact that the energetic understanding is not limited to being officially part of a group recognized as indigenous. This type of conscience is part of the person and is not removed by the mere fact of living outside indigenous territories. This conscience is incompatible with the one/national peace and it is not limited to the essentialist, static and self-contained representation of culture that only exempts indigenous people living in ancestral territories from the duty to perform military service.

Decision C-728/09 shows that supporters of *modern perspectives* on peace (Ministry of Defense in *Decision C-728/09)* interpreted the right to freedom of conscience in accordance to the postulates of modernism. By giving priority to rules of rational logic when building their arguments rather than situations of human suffering, they support hierarchical models of relation and focus on the nation-state as the only meaningful place to express solidarity (Hardt & Negri, 2009).

According to the logic of modern peace advocates, military service is an expression of national solidarity and is *the* essential element for national peace (Presidencia de la República y Ministerio de Defensa de Colombia, 2003; Ministry of Defense in Decision C-728/09). This coincides with Galtung's (1996) account on negative peace based on suppression of conflictive energy. The possibility to object to the use of arms is refused since the national/abstract good is more important than the concrete/contextual good, which appears neglected.

According to this interpretation, only one approach to peace is allowed: the national peace defined by law. An abstract peace based on security is more important than facilitating a concrete situation of peace for the draftee and his family, hence not respecting the right to freedom of conscience is legally justified (Constitutional Court in Decision T-409/92; Presidencia de la República y Ministerio de Defensa de Colombia, 2003; Ministry of Defense in Decision C-728/09).

Interpreters holding *postmodern perspectives* on peace[86] sustained that the multicultural and multiethnic nature of the Colombian society opens possibilities for many (equally valid) perspectives on how to live a good life and how to work collectively for peace. This includes alternative practices of solidarity that will be realized via alternative social services besides the military. Peace is relational and relative; hence the inner peace of the person matters for the law. In this way, it is possible to object to the use of arms for people whose consciencee is perturbed by military service.

This type of interpretation creates "third ways" to overcome the duality (Galtung, 1996) of legal/illegal. This is how petitioners interpreted the constitutional right to equality as a *right to be different* (Petitioners in Decision C-728/09: 6-24). Objections are an expression of pluralism. However, the legal chance to object depends on the draftee's categorization into certain legal categories; it is a rational definition that defines an individual's affiliation to a group who has been legally exempted, like in the case of indigenous people. This is the rational limit of the postmodern perspective.

---

[86] Petitioners, Eafit University, School of Law, Colombian Commission of Jurists (CCJ), UN Human Rights Committee (quoted by petitioners and others), DeJusticia, Professors of Law, Alba Milena Romero supported by War Resisters' International, Conscience and Peace Tax International and Quaker United Nations Office, Colombian Mennonite Church, Centre for Human Rights and International Litigation (CEDHUL), Attorney's General Office of Colombia and Constitutional Court (All in Decision C-728/09).

With regard to the *transrational interpretation*, some intervenors[87] went a step beyond the postmodern. This approach to rights uses the rational but is able to go beyond rational categories. According to them (Anthropology students and others in Decision C-728/09), there is no need to be officially part of a certain ethnicity to express energetic-oriented approaches to peace and subsequent disagreement with militarization.

The anthropology students and others (in Decision C-728/09) coincide with Dietrich's (2008) suggestion to integrate different approaches to deal with peace in a holistic manner. They referred to peace in Colombia in a way that gives importance not only to rational legal arrangements, but also to the human emotional capacities for inclusion and deep respect for life and otherness (Anthropology students and others (in Decision C-728/09).

This is the case of the indigenous people, anthropologists, and conscientious objectors who intervened in the constitutional case. They commented on the importance of using law to respect cultural variations on rights and peace by referring to solidarity beyond the borders of the nation-state. They referred to non-violence as an attitude that needs to be respected, for instance, by the use of legal objections to the use of arms. At the same time, they acknowledged the existence of armies without asking for their elimination. They did not attempt to create a new universal narrative, but genuinely defended the right to freedom of conscience as a tool for respectful coexistence in plurality.

Transrational interpretations of rights will necessarily include the rational legal analysis, taking the sense of order and structure from the modern, pluralism (radical inclusion/non-discrimination) from the postmodern, a sacred sense of human life/dignity from the moral, and lastly, from the energetic, the essential role of the *peace attitude* that makes it possible to harmonize opposites even when reason may speak to the contrary. It can be done when the jurist uses the law along with his/her creativity, compassion, empathy and capacity for transformation. A *relative* and *relational* understanding of the idea of peace in Colombia and its use in legal argumentation are a key element to facilitate *positive peace.* This is an essential contribution from contemporary peace research to the legal theory and practice.

---

[87] Anthropology students Javeriana University and group of objectors, Colombian Collective of Conscientious Objectors (ACOOC) (in Decision C-728/09) and School of Anthropology Andes University (in Decision T-113/09).

REFERENCES

54 International Congress of Americanists "Building Dialogues in the Americas" Vienna, Austria, July 15 – 20, 2012. See http://ica2012.univie.ac.at/

Alchourrón, C., & Bulygin, E. (2006). *Introducción a la metodología de las ciencias jurídicas y sociales*. Buenos Aires: Astrea.

Alessandri R., Vodanovic H., A., & Somarriva U., M. (1998). *Tratado de derecho civil: partes preliminar y general*. Santiago: Editorial Jurídica de Chile.

Anderson, B. (2006). *Imagined communities: reflections on the origin and spread of nationalism*. London, New York: Verso.

Anncol (2010). *El costo silenciado de la operación Sodoma*. Retrieved October 7, 2010, from http://anncol.eu/paracio-narino/5/el-costo-silenciado-de-la-operacion-sodoma964.

Arendt, H. (1966). *The origins of totalitarianism*. New York: Harcourt, Brace & World.

Arendt, H. (2005). *Ensayos de comprensión 1930-1954*. Madrid: Caparrós.

Arendt, H. (2006). *Eichmann in Jerusalem: a report on the banality of evil*. Los Angeles: Topeka Bindery.

Aristizabal, H., & Lefer, D. (2010). *The Blessing Next to the Wound: A Story of Art, Activism, and Transformation*. New York: Lantern Books.

Assagioli, R. (1927). *A new method of healing: psychosynthesis*. London: Institute of Psychosynthesis.

Atienza, M. (1985). *Introducción al Derecho*. Barcelona: Barcanova.

Atienza, M. (1999). *El Derecho como Argumentación*. Isegoría, Revista de Filosofía Moral y Política, 21, 37-47. Retrieved August 31, 2010, from http://isegoria.revistas.csic.es/index.php/isegoria/article/viewFile/76/76.

Atienza, M. (2000). *Tres lecciones de teoría del derecho*. Alicante: Club Universitario.

Atienza, M. (2006). *El derecho como argumentación: concepciones de la argumentación*. Barcelona: Ariel.

Atienza, M., & Ruiz, J. (1991). *Sobre principios y reglas*. Doxa: Cuadernos de Filosofía del Derecho, 10, 101-120. Retrieved August 30, 2010, from http://www.cervantesvirtual.com/servlet/SirveObras/12482196462352624198846/cuaderno10/doxa10_04.pdf.

Austin, J. (2009). *Lectures on jurisprudence or the philosophy of positive law*, Volume 1. Charleston: BiblioBazaar, LLC.

Ávila, H. (2007). *Theory of legal principles*. Dordrecht: Springer.

Banham, M. (1998). *The Cambridge guide to theatre*. Cambridge: Cambridge University Press.

Barraca Mairal, J. (2005). *Pensar el Derecho: curso de filosofía jurídica*. Madrid: Ediciones Palabra.

BBC News. (2009). *Toxic fallout of Colombian scandal*. London. Retrieved May 18, 2011, from http://news.bbc.co.uk/2/hi/americas/8038399.stm.

Bender, H. S. (1955). *Excommunication*. Global Anabaptist Mennonite Encyclopedia Online. Retrieved April 11, 2011, from http://www.gameo.org/encyclopedia/contents/E948.html.

Bentham, J. (1823). *An introduction to the principles of morals and legislation*, Volume 1. London: W. Pickering.

Bernard, V., Ottemberg, P., & Redl, F. (2003). *Dehumanization: a composite psychological defense in relation to modern war*. In M. Schwebel (Ed.), Behavioral Science and Human Survival (pp. 64-83). Bloomington: iUniverse.

Boal, A. (2000). *Theater of the Oppressed*. Pluto Classics Series. Pluto.

Bobbio, N. (1998). *Diccionario de política: a-j*. Coyoacán: Siglo XXI.

Botero, Á. (2006). *La esfera inconclusa: novela colombiana en el ámbito global*. Medellín: Universidad de Antioquia.

Boulding, E. (2000). *Cultures of peace: the hidden side of history*. New York: Syracuse University Press.

Bouris, E. (2007). *Complex Political Victims*: Bloomfield: Kumarian Press.

Brook, T. (2007). *Vermeer's hat: the seventeenth century and the dawn of the global world*. London: Bloomsbury Press.

Brownlee, K. (2007). *Civil disobedience*. Stanford Encyclopedia of Philosophy. Retrieved February 11, 2011, from http://plato.stanford.edu/entries/civil-disobedience/.

Brownlee, K. (2012). *Conscience and Conviction: The Case for Civil Disobedience*. Oxford Legal Philosophy. OUP Oxford.

Bugental, J. F. T., Schneider, K. J., & Pierson, J. F. (2001). *The Handbook of Humanistic Psychology: Leading Edges in Theory, Research, and Practice*: SAGE Publications.

Butler, J. (2006). *Precarious life: the powers of mourning and violence*. London-New York: Verso.

CNP - Consejo Nacional de Planeación. (2010). *Seguridad Democrática: balance de ocho años*. Bogotá. In file with author.

CODHES - Consultoría para los Derechos Humanos y el Desplazamiento (2011). *De la seguridad a la prosperidad democrática en medio del conflicto* (Documento CODHES n. 23). Bogotá: Antropos.

Cohen, D. B. (2009). *I Carry Your Heart in My Heart: Family Constellations in Prison*. Heidelberg: Carl Auer.

Constitución Política de Colombia. (1991). Bogotá: Asamblea Nacional Constituyente de Colombia. Retrieved October 18, 2010, from http://web.presidencia.gov.co/constitucion/index.pdf.

Constitution of Colombia. (1991). Bogotá: National Constituent Assembly of Colombia. Translation available at the University of Richmond's web site. Retrieved July 8, 2010 from http://confinder.richmond.edu/admin/docs/colombia_const2.pdf.

Convention on the Rights of the Child. (1989). United Nations General Assembly. Retrieved October 7, 2010, from http://www2.ohchr.org/english/law/crc.htm.

Cortázar, J. (1963). *Rayuela*. Buenos Aires: Sudamericana.

Decree-Law 100/80. (1980) *"Por el cual se expide el Código Penal" (abrogated)*. Bogotá: Government of Colombia. Retrieved October 17, 2010, from http://www.icbf.gov.co/transparencia/derechobienestar/codigo/codigo_penal_1980_pr009.html.

Deleuze, G., & Guattari, F. (2004). *A thousand plateaus: capitalism and schizophrenia*. London-New York: Continuum International Publishing Group.

Desision C-027/93. (1993). Bogotá: Colombian Constitutional Court. Judge Rapporteur: Simón Rodríguez Rodríguez.

Desision C-058/94. (1994). Bogotá: Colombian Constitutional Court. Judge-Rapporteur: Alejandro Martinez Caballero.

Desision C-370/06. (2006). Bogotá: Colombian Constitutional Court. Judge Rapporteur: Manuel José Cepeda Espinosa, Jaime Córdoba Triviño, Rodrigo Escobar Gil, Marco Gerardo Monroy Cabra, Álvaro Tafur Galvis, Clara Inés Vargas Hernández.

Desision C-511/94. (1994). Bogotá: Colombian Constitutional Court. Judge-Rapporteur: Fabio Morón Díaz.

Desision C-659/97. (1997). Bogotá: Colombian Constitutional Court. Judge-Rapporteur: José Gregorio Hernández Galindo.

Desision C-728/09. (2009). Bogotá: Colombian Constitutional Court. Judge-Rapporteur: Gabriel Eduardo Mendoza Martelo.

Desision C-740/01. (2001). Bogotá: Colombian Constitutional Court. Judge Rapporteur: Álvaro Tafur Galvis.

Desision T-113/09. (2009). Bogotá: Colombian Constitutional Court. Judge Rapporteur: Clara Elena Reales Gutiérrez.

Desision T-209/08. (2008). Bogotá: Colombian Constitutional Court. Judge Rapporteur: Clara Inés Vargas Hernández.

Desision T-363/95. (1995). Bogotá: Colombian Constitutional Court. Judge-Rapporteur: José Gregorio Hernández Galindo.

Desision T-409/92. (1992). Bogotá: Colombian Constitutional Court. Judge-Rapporteur: José Gregorio Hernández Galindo.

Desision T-537/93. (1993). Bogotá: Colombian Constitutional Court.

Desision T-588/98. (1998). Bogotá: Colombian Constitutional Court. Judge-Rapporteur: Eduardo Cifuentes Muñoz.

Desision T-982/01. (2001). Bogotá: Colombian Constitutional Court. Judge-Rapporteur: Manuel José Cepeda.

Devis Echandía, H. (2004). *Teoría general del proceso. Aplicable a toda clase de procesos*. Buenos Aires: Universidad.

Diamond, D. (2007). *Theatre for Living: The Art and Science of Community-Based Dialogue*. Trafford Publishing.

Diamond, D. (2007). *Theatre for Living: The Art and Science of Community-Based Dialogue*. Trafford Publishing.

Dietrich, W. (2000). *A structural-cyclic model of developments in human rights*. Retrieved October 15, 2010, from http://www.du.edu/korbel/hrhw/workingpapers/1999-2001/06-dietrich-04-00.pdf.

Dietrich, W. (2006a). *A call for transrational peaces*. Retrieved May 24, 2010, from http://www.uibk.ac.at/peacestudies/downloads/peacelibrary/transrational.pdf

Dietrich, W. (2006b). *Peaces: an aesthetic concept, a moral need or a transrational virtue?* *Asteriskos. Journal of international Peace Studies, 1/2, 25-46.

Dietrich, W. (2008). *Variationen über die Vielen Frieden. Band 1: Deutungen.* Wiesbaden: VS-Verlag.

Dietrich, W. (2009). *La llamada a las paces transracionales*. Cátedra magistral dictada el 20 de Abril de 2009 en la Universidad de los Andes en Mérida (Venezuela) dentro del marco del I Encuentro Internacional de Arte, Paz y Sustenibilidad: http://www.eventos.ula.ve/artepazsustentabilidad

Dietrich, W. (2012). *Interpretations of peace in history and culture*, London: Palgrave Macmillan.

Dietrich, W., & Sützl, W. (1997). "A call for many peaces". Schlaining papers. Retrieved March 12, 2011, from http://www.aspr.ac.at/publications/wp7_97.pdf.

Dietrich, W., & Sützl, W. (2006). "A call for many peaces". In W. Dietrich, J. Echavarría & N. Koppensteiner (Eds.), *Key Texts of Peace Studies* (pp. 282-301). Vienna: LIT Verlag.

Dietrich, W., Echavarría, J., Esteva, G., Ingruber, D., & Koppensteiner, N. (Eds.). (2011). *The Palgrave international handbook of peace studies: a cultural perspective*. London: Palgrave Macmillan.

Drucker, T. (2008). *Perspectives on the history of mathematical logic*. Carlisle: Birkhäuser.

Dworkin, R. (1977). *Taking rights seriously*. Cambridge: Harvard University Press.

Dworkin, R. (1996). *Freedom's law: the moral reading of the American Constitution*. New York: Oxford University Press.

Echavarría, J. (2010). *In/Security in Colombia: Writing Political Identities in the Democratic Security Policy*. Manchester: Manchester University Press.

Echavarría, J. (2011). *Revisiting the concept of solidarity: support and collaboration networks in Colombia*. Conference script (unpublished). Left Forum: Toward a Politics of Solidarity. March 2011. New York.

Ejército Nacional de Colombia. (2009). *El Ejército lanza comerciales con la marca "Los héroes en Colombia sí existen"*. Retrieved March 5, 2011, from http://www.ejercito.mil.co/?idcategoria=228782.

El Colombiano. (2010). *Sacha es un soldado irremplazable*. September 24, 2010. Medellín. Retrieved October 17, 2010, from http://www.elcolombiano.com/BancoConocimiento/S/sacha_es_un_soldado_irremplazable/sacha_es_un_soldado_irremplazable.asp.

El Espectador. (2010). *"Esta es mi bienvenida a las Farc": Santos*. September 23, 2010. Bogotá. Retrieved October 7, 2010, from http://www.elespectador.com/noticias/judicial/articulo-225757-cayo-el-mono-jojoy.

El Tiempo. (2010a). *¿Cómo nos matamos?* May 8, 2010. Bogotá. Retrieved February 21, 2011, from http://www.eltiempo.com/archivo/documento/CMS-7699653.

El Tiempo. (2010b). *Lo que opinan los ciudadanos sobre la muerte del "Mono Jojoy"*. September 23, 2010. Bogotá. Retrieved October 7, 2010, from http://www.eltiempo.com/archivo/documento/CMS-7963820.

Encyclopedia Britannica. (2010). *Rhizome (plant anatomy)*. Retrieved June 3, 2010, from http://www.britannica.com/EBchecked/topic/501483/rhizome.

Engle, E. (2010). "Taking the Right Seriously: Hohfeldian Semiotics and Rights Discourse". *The Crit*, 3(1), 84-107. Retrieved August 18, 2010, from http://www.thecritui.com/articles/Engle II.pdf.

Erikson, E. (1995). *A way of looking at things: selected papers from 1930 to 1980*. New York: Norton.

Espinoza, L. (2001). *Primeras reflexiones sobre una pedagogía postmoderna para Latinoamérica*. Ponencia presentada en mesa redonda del Congreso Pedagogía 2001, La Habana, Cuba. Revista Extramuros N° 1. Retrieved April 16, 2011, from http://www.umce.cl/revistas/extramuros/extramuros_n01_a07.html#ponencia.

Esteva, G., & Prakash, M.(1998). *Grassroots post-modernism: remaking the soil of cultures*. Basingstoke: Palgrave Macmillan.

Falcón y Tella, M., & Muckley, P. (2004). *Civil disobedience*. Boston: Martinus Nijhoff.

Frank, J. (1973). *Courts on trial: myth and reality in American justice*. Princeton: Princeton University Press.

Friedman, L. (2000). *Identity's architect: a biography of Erik H. Erikson*. Cambridge: Harvard University Press.

Fuentes, C. (1962). *La muerte de Artemio Cruz*. Madrid: Fondo de Cultura Económica de España.

Fuenzalida, N., & Fuenzalida, M. (2007). *Un postmodernismo Latinoamericano*. Retrieved July 8, 2010, from http://laresearchinstitute.blogspot.com/2007/09/un-postmodernismo-latino-americano_18.html.

Galtung, J. (1990). "Cultural violence". *Journal of Peace Research, Sage*. Retrieved July 9, 2010, from http://www.okan.edu.tr/.

Galtung, J. (1996). *Peace by peaceful means: peace and conflict, development and civilization*. Oslo: Sage.

García Márquez, G. (1967). *Cien años de soledad*. Buenos Aires: Sudamericana.

Goodman, P. (1962). *Growing up absurd: problems of youth in the organized society*. New York: Vintage.

Grosz, E. (2001). *Architecture from the Outside: Essays on Virtual and Real Space*. MIT Press.

Gupta, A., & Ferguson, J. (1992). *Beyond culture: space, identity, and politics of difference*. Cultural Anthropology, Vol. 7(1), 6-23.

Gyatso, T. —14th Dalai Lama—. (1988). *"The 14th Dalai Lama - Nobel Lecture"*. Nobelprize.org. Retrieved September 27, 2010 from http://nobelprize.org/nobel_prizes/peace/laureates/1989/lama-lecture.html

Hall, S. (1996). "Who needs identity?" In S. Hall & P. Du Gay (Eds.), *Questions of cultural identity*. London: Sage.

Hansen, P. (1993). *Hannah Arendt: politics, history and citizenship.* Palo Alto: Stanford University Press.

Hardt, M., & Negri, A. (2009). *Commonwealth*. Cambridge: Belknap Press of Harvard University Press.

Hart, H. (1961). *The concept of law*. Gloucestershire: Clarendon Press.

Hart, H. (1983). *Essays in jurisprudence and philosophy*. Oxford: Oxford University Press.

Heidegger, M. (1973). *The end of philosophy and the task of thinking*. (Translated and with an Introduction by Joan Stambaugh, Eds.). Chicago: University of Chicago Press.

Heidegger, M., & Sadler, T. (2002). *The essence of truth: on Plato's cave allegory and theaetetus*. New York, London: Continuum International Publishing Group.

Hellinger, B. (2002). *On Life & Other Paradoxes: Aphorisms and Little Stories from Bert Hellinger*. Phoenix, Arizona: Zeig Tucker & Theisen.

Hellinger, B. (2003). *Farewell: family constellations with descendants of victims and perpetrators*. Heidelberg: Carl-Auer-Systeme Verlag & Verlagsbuchhandlung GmbH.

Hoelzl, M. (2004). "Recognizing the sacrificial victim: the problem of solidarity for critical social theory". *Journal for Cultural and Religious Theory*, 6(1), 45-64. Retrieved May 19, 2011, from http://www.jcrt.org/archives/06.1/hoelzl.pdf.

Hoover, K. (2004). *The future of identity: centennial reflections on the legacy of Erik Erikson*. Lanham: Lexington Books.

Horowitz, A., & Horowitz, G. (2006). *Difficult justice: commentaries on Levinas and politics*. Toronto: University of Toronto Press.

Huertas, M. (2006). *Do critical international legal studies effectively deny the existence of a positive international law?* Retrieved August 4, 2010, from http://www.reei.org/reei 12/HuertasJimenez(reei12).pdf.

Human Rights Educators' Network, Amnesty International USA, (1998). *A short history of human rights*. Retrieved October 14, 2010, from http://www1.umn.edu/humanrts/edumat/hreduseries/hereandnow/Part-1/short-history.htm.

Huntington, S. (1997). "The real world: the civilizations shaping the new global order". Adapted from University at Buffalo map collection, from: "The Many Faces of the Future: Why We'll Never Have a Universal Civilization" *Utne Reader* (May/June 1997): 76. Retrieved May 14, 2011, from http://library.buffalo.edu/maps/mapresources/mapsinnewsarticles.php.

Illich, I. (1982). *Vom Recht auf die Gemeinheit*. Reinbek: Rowohlt.

Illich, I. (2006). "Peace vs. Development". In W. Dietrich, J. Echavarría & N. Koppensteiner (Eds.), *Key Texts of Peace Studies* (pp. 173-182). Vienna: LIT Verlag.

IMF - International Monetary Fund (2008). *World Economic Outlook Database*, April 2008. Retrieved 5 October, 2012, from http://www.imf.org/external/pubs/ft/weo/2008/01/weodata/index.aspx

IMF - International Monetary Fund (2012). *World Economic Outlook Database*, April 2012. Retrieved 5 October, 2012, from http://www.imf.org/external/pubs/ft/weo/2012/01/weodata/weoselco.aspx?g=110&sg=All+countries+%2f+Advanced+economies

Infante, G. (1990). *Tres tristes tigres*. Caracas: Fundación Biblioteca Ayacucho.

INMLCF - Instituto Nacional de Medicina Legal y Ciencias Forenses. (2009). Reporte de datos oficiales sobre la violencia en Colombia. *Informe Forensis: datos de vida*. Retrieved February 21, 2011, from http://www.medicinalegal.gov.co/index.php?option=com_wrapper&view=wrapper&Itemid=60.

Inwood, M. (1992). *A Hegel dictionary*. Malden, Massachusetts: Wiley-Blackwell.

Jaramillo, S., Giha, Y., & Torres, P. (2009). *Transitional Justice and DDR: The Case of Colombia*. International Center for Transitional Justice (ICTJ).

Jung, C. (1969). *The archetypes and the collective unconscious*. (Vol. 9, p. 451). Princeton: Princeton University Press.

Kelsen, H. (1978). *Pure theory of law*. Berkeley -London: University of California Press.

Kennedy, D. (1990). *Legal education as training for hierarchy: The politics of law*. Retrieved August 10, 2010, from http://duncankennedy.net/documents/Legal Education as Training for Hierarchy_Politics of Law.pdf.

Kennedy, D. (2002). "The critique of rights in critical legal studies". In Brown And Halley (Eds.), *Left Legalism/Left Critique* (pp. 178-227). Duke University Press. Retrieved September 28, 2010, from http://duncankennedy.net/documents/The Critique of Rights in cls.pdf.

Kennedy, D., & Carrington, P. (2004). *Legal education and the reproduction of hierarchy: a polemic against the system*. New York: New York University Press.

Konrad-Adenauer-Stiftung. Oficina Colombia. (2008). *¿Conflicto interno armado o amenaza terrorista?* Retrieved March 5, 2011, from http://www.kas.de/kolumbien/es/publications/12988/.

Koppensteiner, N. (2009). *The art of the transpersonal self: transformation as aesthetic and energetic practice*. New York-Dresden: Atropos Press.

Koppensteiner, N. (2010). *Trans-rational Interpretations of Peace*. Lecture. Innsbruck, January 2010: MA Program for Peace, Development, Security and International Conflict Transformation. University of Innsbruck.

La Noticia. (2010). *En Colombia, aumento en casos de homicidio: se pasó de 15.250 asesinatos en el 2008 a 17.717*. May 6, 2010. Cali. Retrieved March 7, 2011, from http://goyes.wordpress.com/2010/05/06/en-colombia-aumento-casos-de-homicidio-se-paso-de-15-250-asesinatos-en-el-2008-a-17-717/.

Larraín, J. (1996). *Postmodernismo e identidad latinoamericana*. Escritos, Revista del Centro de Ciencias del Lenguaje, 13-14, 45-74.

Law 1448/11. (2011). "Por la cual se dictan medidas de atención, asistencia y reparación integral a las víctimas del conflicto armado interno y se dictan otras disposiciones" Bogotá: Colombian Congress. June 10, 2011. Retreived September 30, 2012, from http://www.mij.gov.co/Ministerio/Library/News/Files/CARTILLA%20LEY%20DE%20V%C3%8DCTIMAS%20Y%20RESTITUCI%C3%93N%20DE%20TIERRAS70.PDF

Law 48/93. (1993). *"Por la cual se reglamenta el servicio de Reclutamiento y Movilización"*. Bogotá: Colombian Congress. March 03, 1993. Retrieved January 21, 2011, from http://www.secretariasenado.gov.co/senado/basedoc/ley/1993/ley_0048_1993.html.

Lederach, J. P. (1997). *Building peace: sustainable reconciliation in divided societies*. Washington: US Institute of Peace Press.

Lemaitre, J. (2011). *La paz en cuestión: La guerra y la paz en la Asamblea Constituyente de 1991*. Bogotá: Universidad de los Andes.

Lozano, N. (2012). *Playing music, performing resistance: The dynamics of resistance through music in the Colombian south Pacific Coast*. Vienna-Berlin: Lit Verlag.

Luis, W., & González, A. (1994). *Modern Latin-American fiction writers*. Dictionary of Literary Biography, Volume 145. Gale Research International Limited.

Lyotard, J. F. (1984). *The postmodern condition: a report on knowledge*. Minneapolis: University of Minnesota Press.

Malagón, M. (2011). "La regeneración, la constitución de 1886 y el papel de la iglesia católica". *Revista electrónica de difusión científica – Universidad Sergio Arboleda*, 11. Retrieved March 20, 2011, from http://www.usergioarboleda.edu.co/civilizar/revista11/regeneracion_constitucion.pdf.

Maslow, A. (1943). "A theory of human motivation". *Psychological Review*, 50(4), 370-396. BYU Electronic Media Dept.

Maslow, A. (1971). *The farther reaches of human nature*. New York: Viking Press.

Maslow, A. (1999). *Toward a psychology of being*. Hoboken: J. Wiley & Sons.

Máynez, E. (1974). *Filosofía del derecho*. México D.F.: Porrúa.

Ministerio de Defensa Nacional - República de Colombia. (2010). *Rueda de prensa del Ministro de Defensa, Rodrigo Rivera Salazar, sobre la muerte en combate de alias "el mono jojoy."* Bogotá. Retrieved March 21, 2011, from http://www.mindefensa.gov.co/irj/go/km/docs/documents/News/NoticiaGrandeMDN/400b93a9-55a9-2d10-1eb0-ab585cbfc6e2.xml.

Ministerio de Defensa Nacional – República de Colombia. (2011). *Política Integral de Seguridad y Defensa para la Prosperidad*. Retrieved 29 September, 2012, from http://www.fac.mil.co/recursos_user/documentos/Politica.pdf

Moskos, C., & Chambers, J. (1993). *The New conscientious objection: from sacred to secular resistance*. New York: Oxford University Press.

Muñoz I., C. (Ed.). (1998). *Calidad, Equidad y Eficacia de la Educación Primaria: Estado Actual de las Investigaciones Realizadas en América Latina*. Santiago: Cee-reduc-cide.

Muñoz, F (2006). "Imperfect peace". In W. Dietrich, J. Echavarría & N. Koppensteiner (Eds.), *Ke*

Nanclares, A. (2001). *Los jueces de mármol*. Medellín: La Pisca Tabaca.

Nieto, A., & Fernández, T. (1998). *El derecho y el revés: diálogo epistolar sobre leyes, abogados y jueces*. Madrid: Ariel.

Nietzsche, F. (2007). *Die Geburt der Tragödie: Aus dem Geiste der Musik* [*The birth of tragedy from the Spirit of Music*]. Cambridge: Cambridge University Press.

Nino, C. (1980a). *Introducción al análisis del derecho*. Buenos Aires: Astrea.

Nino, C. (1980b). "Dworkin and legal positivism". *Mind*, LXXXIX, 519-543. Retrieved February 14, 2011, from http://mind.oxfordjournals.org/content/LXXXIX/356/519.full.pdf.

Orozco, I. (2005). "Reflexiones impertinentes: sobre la memoria y el olvido, sobre el castigo y la clemencia". In A. Rettberg (Ed.), *Entre el Perdón y el Paredón: Preguntas y Dilemas de la Justicia Transicional* (pp. 171-210). Bogotá: Universidad de Los Andes.

Parker, C. (1973). *Otra Lógica en América Latina: religión popular y modernización capitalista*. Santiago: Fondo de la Cultura Económica.

Pérez, G. (2010). "De la Seguridad Democrática a la Prosperidad Democrática" Razón Pública. 15 August 2010. Retrieved 5 October 2012, from http://razonpublica.com/index.php/politica-y-gobierno-temas-27/1277-de-la-seguridad-democratica-a-la-prosperidad-democratica.html

Portafolio. (2010). *Colombia incrementó un 11% el gasto militar en el 2009 y Venezuela fue la que más lo redujo, según estudio.* June 1, 2010. Bogotá. Retrieved March 5, 2011, from http://www.portafolio.com.co/archivo/documento/CMS-7735146.

Posada, J., & Álvarez, J. (2010). *El eterno misterio de las tumbas guerrilleras*. El Colombiano. September 25, 2010. Medellín. Retrieved October 7, 2010, from http://www.elcolombiano.com/BancoConocimiento/E/el_eterno_misterio_de_las_tumbas_guerrilleras/el_eterno_misterio_de_las_tumbas_guerrilleras.asp?CodSeccion=267.

Presidencia de la República y Ministerio de Defensa de Colombia. (2003). *Política de Defensa y Seguridad Democrática*. Retrieved March 1, 2011, from http://www.presidencia.gov.co/seguridad_democratica.pdf.

Procuraduría General de la Nación, República de Colombia. (2011). Official website. Retrieved February 20, 2011, from http://www.procuraduria.gov.co/html/infoinstitucional/infoinst_quehacemos.htm.

Rawls, J. (1971). *A Theory of Justice*. Cambridge: Harvard University Press.

Reece, H. (1998). *Law and science*. New York: Oxford University Press.

Resolution 1879/01. (2001). Bogotá: Ministerio de Defensa Nacional de Colombia.

Resolution 1987/46. (1989). United Nations Human Rights Commission.

Resolution 1998/77. (1998). United Nations Human Rights Commission.

Resolution 33/165. (1978). United Nations General Assembly.

Rosenberg, M. (2003). *Nonviolent communication: a language of life*. Encinitas: PuddleDancer.

Ross, A. (2004). *On law and justice*. New Jersey: The Lawbook Exchange.

Semana. (2009). *Las cuentas de los falsos positivos*. January 27, 2009. Bogotá. Retrieved May 18, 2011, from http://www.semana.com/justicia/cuentas-falsos-positivos/120116-3.aspx.

Semana. (2010). *Golpe al terror*. September 25, 2010. Bogotá. Retrieved October 7, 2010, from http://www.semana.com/noticias-nacion/golpe-terror/145134.aspx.

Semana. (2011a). *Intolerancia*. February 26, 2011. Bogotá. Retrieved March 2, 2011, from http://www.semana.com/noticias-nacion/intolerancia/152473.aspx.

Semana. (2011b). *Pérez Esquivel: "Uribe tiene que dar cuenta de muchas cosas"*. February 24, 2011. Bogotá. Retrieved March 1, 2011, from http://www.semana.com/noticias-nacion/perez-esquivel-uribe-tiene-dar-cuenta-muchas-cosas/152328.aspx.

Singer, P. (1973). *Democracy and disobedience.* Oxford: Clarendon Press.

Skeat, W. (1993). *The concise dictionary of English etymology.* Hertfordshire: Wordsworth.

Sophocles. (2008). *The Antigone*. Charleston, SC: BiblioBazaar, LLC.

Spinosa, C., Flores, F., & Dreyfus, H. (1999). *Disclosing new worlds: entrepreneurship, democratic action, and the cultivation of solidarity.* Cambridge: Massachusetts Institute of Technology (MIT) Press.

Stanford Encyclopedia of Philosophy. (2008). *Self-reference*. Retrieved June 3, 2010, from http://plato.stanford.edu/entries/self-reference/.

Strozier, C. B., & Flynn, M. (1996). *Genocide, war, and human survival*. Lanham: Rowman & Littlefield.

Suárez, E. (2002). *Introducción al derecho*. Santa Fe: Publicaciones Universidad Nacional del Litoral.

Sunkel, G. (1988). *Representations of the people in the Chilean popular press*. Unpublished PhD Thesis. University of Birmingham.

Takemura, H. (2009). *International human right to conscientious objection to military service and individual duties to disobey manifestly illegal orders*. Berlin: Springer.

Tamanaha, B. Z. (2004). *On the rule of law: history, politics, theory*. New York: Cambridge University Press.

Thoreau, H. D. (1993). *Civil Disobedience and Other Essays*: Dover Publications.

UN Human Rights Committee. (2004). *Observaciones finales del Comité de Derechos Humanos: Colombia*. 26/05/2004. CCPR/CO/80/COL. (Concluding Observations/Comments). Retrieved February 18, 2011, from http://www.unhchr.ch/tbs/doc.nsf/(Symbol)/CCPR.CO.80.COL.Sp?Opendocument.

UN Human Rights Committee. (2007). CCPR/C/88/D/1321-1322/2004, Mr. *Yeo-Bum Yoon and Mr. Myung-Jin Choi vs. Republic of Korea* (Jurisprudence). Retrieved February 10, 2011, from http://www.unhchr.ch/tbs/doc.nsf/(Symbol)/26a8e9722d0cdadac1257279004c1b4e?Opendocument.

UN Security Council. (2004). *The rule of law and transitional justice in conflict and post-conflict societies*. Report (S/2004/616). Retrieved October 1, 2010, from http://www.un.org/en/ruleoflaw/index.shtml.

Universal Declaration of Human Rights. (1948). United Nations General Assembly. Retrieved October 4, 2010, from http://www.un.org/en/documents/udhr/.

Universität Innsbruck. (2011). The MA Program for Peace Studies. About the Program, the Philosophy of the Many Peaces. Retrieved April 11, 2011, from http://www.uibk.ac.at/peacestudies/ma-program/about/.

UNOHCHR - United Nations Office of the High Commissioner for Human Rights in Colombia. (2006). *Report on human rights.*

UNOHCHR - United Nations Office of the High Commissioner for Human Rights in Colombia. (2009). *Report on human rights.*

Vargas Llosa, M. (1968). *La casa verde*. Barcelona: Seix Barral.

Vattimo, G. (2006). "Dialectics, difference and weak thought". In W. Dietrich, J. Echavarría & N. Koppensteiner (Eds.), *Key Texts of Peace Studies* (pp. 227-241). Viena: LIT Verlag Münster.

Vecchio, G. (1946). *Filosofía del derecho*, Volume 1. México D.F: Unión Tip. Editorial Hispano-Americana.

War Resisters' International. (2009). *Military recruitment and conscientious objection in Colombia*. Retrieved March 7, 2011, from http://www.wri-irg.org/es/node/8442.

Wilber, K. (1995). *Sex, ecology, spirituality: the spirit of evolution*. Boston: Shambhala.

Wilber, K. (2000). *Integral psychology: consciousness, spirit, psychology, therapy*. Boston: Shambhala.

Wilber, K. (2007). A *brief history of everything*. Boston: Shambhala Publications.

Wiles, D. (1997). *Tragedy in Athens, performance space and theatrical meaning*. Cambridge: Cambridge University Press.

William W. Fisher, I., Horwitz, M. J., & Reed, T. A. (1993). *American Legal Realism*. Oxford University Press.

y Texts for Peace Studies (pp. 241-282). Vienna: LIT Verlag.

Zimbardo, P. (2008). *The Lucifer effect: understanding how good people turn evil*. New York: Random House.

Žižek, S. (2011). *For Egypt, this is the miracle of Tahrir square*. The Guardian. 10 February 2011. London. Retrieved February 11, 2011, from http://www.guardian.co.uk/global/2011/feb/10/egypt-miracle-tahrir-square